KV-085-057

Tracing My Journey

MARGARET AHERN NOONAN

RED HEN PUBLISHING

First published in 2010 by
Red Hen Publishing
Duagh, Listowel
Co Kerry, Ireland
Email: redhen1@eircom.net
+00353 (0)68 45942

Typesetting and design by Jane Stark
seamistgraphics@gmail.com

Printed in Spain by GraphyCems

Copyright © 2010 Margaret Ahern Noonan

All rights reserved. No part of this publication may be reproduced
or used in any form or by any means – photographic, electronic
or mechanical, including photocopying, recording, taping or
information storage and retrieval systems – without the prior
permission of the publisher in writing.

ISBN 978-0-9552920-6-4

A catalogue record of this book
is available from the British Library

In loving memory of my parents,
Sarah and Paddy,
my sister, Patricia (Pat),
and my brother, Pa

Thou hast traced my journey
and my resting places
and art familiar with my paths

Psalm 139

CONTENTS

ACKNOWLEDGEMENTS

My sincere thanks to all of my family for their help and support throughout my life; to my niece Patricia Danaher for encouraging me to write my life story, to Sister Eileen for being such a wonderful friend, to Dan O'Connor for all his help and encouragement, to Paddy Kennelly for showing such faith in my story, and to my husband, Bill, for being a wonderful presence in my life each and every day.

FOREWORD

At the age of 15 Margaret Ahern left the warmth and security of her family home in Athea, County Limerick, and entered the novitiate at the Presentation Convent in Castleconnell, County Limerick. Her work as a nun would take her from Ireland to England and eventually to Rhodesia (now Zimbabwe) where she would work for many years as a nurse before returning to Ireland where she would leave convent life and marry Bill Noonan, the man she loved.

Margaret's story is one of courage sustained through the most daunting challenges. In lucid and simple prose she details her encounters with homesickness and with the lonely seclusion of convent life. While she expertly captures the scenic beauty of Zimbabwe, the most striking impression, for the reader, is of a land ravaged by the injustices of racial segregation, leading at last to insurrection and widespread violence. This violence was indiscriminate and life-threatening. Margaret was witness to the deaths of friends and colleagues, victims of this violence.

She herself was close to being killed many times. She drove over roads pocked with landmines, and miraculously survived. She hid all night from insurgents who sought her death. Through it all her courage never failed. Only when it became impossible for her to stay did she leave her post and the people for whom she had toiled unceasingly.

Margaret's story is also the story of the Hidden Church. This is the Church of Christ's followers who toil without seeking reward and minister to the poor and underprivileged, far from acclaim or public recognition. It is the Church which goes about its charitable work daily, unobtrusively and unacknowledged. It is the Church that, even as you read this, is busy at its ministry of love.

Margaret Ahern's story is one well worth the telling and well worth the reading.

Paddy Kennelly
(A Place Too Small for Secrets and *Disciples)*

EARLY YEARS

Direen, Athea, County Limerick

1934-1949

I grew up on a small farm in rural Ireland in the townland of Direen, Athea, in west Limerick. My childhood years were the happiest years of my life and, looking back on that time, I realise how blessed and how lucky we were to be reared in a rural area, where life was peaceful and happy and where we were very close to nature. My father, Paddy Ahern, spent his life farming and inherited the farm from his father. My mother, Sarah McElligott, lived in England for some years where she worked as a teacher. She returned to Ireland and, while travelling with her sister, who was a midwife, she met my father. They fell in love and got married and were blessed with a healthy, happy family of six girls and one boy. Older than me were Mary Agnes, Eileen, Patrick (known as Pa) and Sheila, and younger than me were Bridie and Patricia (known as Pat).

My very earliest memories go back to the time when we left our old house to go to a new house which my father and other relations had built. The transition was a difficult time for me and I was constantly asking my mother when were we going back home. On her trips to the well for water she would take me with her as we passed by the old house en route. We grew up in a very close-knit family and, as we got older, we became familiar with the different aspects of farm life, such as cutting the hay in summer time. I can remember working in the meadow in the lovely summer weather when we, dressed in our summer dresses, turned and twisted the hay as it began to dry out and turn a lovely golden colour. A few days later it would be put into heaps. Later it was put into wynds, which were large heaps of hay that were brought to a point at the top and raked to weather-proof them. The wynds took some time to dry completely before being drawn into the hay barn.

What I associate most with the meadow were the lovely apple cakes that my mother would make for the tea. They were juicy, with lots of sugar and apples bursting out of them. That, with a good mug of tea, was indeed food for a king. Also at that time of the year, turf was cut in the peat bog. For us it was a backbreaking chore but the best fun was also to be had in the bog where we worked from the time we were knee-high. It was a great time for chat, laughter, storytelling and eating wholesome food, which never tasted as good anywhere else as it did in the bog.

Apart from helping with the hay and the turf, there were lots of other chores that we as children were able to help out with. The fowl, including hens, chickens, turkeys and a few geese, had to be fed and put into their own secure houses by night in case a marauding fox came prowling. The problem with the fox was that he did not just kill enough to feed his hunger; the fox would slaughter every bird in the nest. The fowl reared on the family farm were a source of many a lovely Sunday dinner as well as providing eggs for breakfast in the mornings, served with a slice of home-cured bacon. At that time most farmers would fatten and kill a pig, which would provide enough bacon for almost a full year. A day was set aside for killing the pig which was a ritual in itself and, as such, required a good deal of planning. There was one man in our area who volunteered for that work with joy – I think the reason was that he knew that on his homeward journey he would be carrying a good supply of pork products.

For the woman of the house such a day meant a lot of extra work as there was the tradition of making black puddings to be upheld, and neighbours would help with the preparations as was the custom of the time. All the necessary ingredients had to be prepared the day before the killing. Once the puddings had dried out a bit, the frying pan was out and, with a piece of pork-steak and black pudding, a delicious meal was enjoyed by us all. It was customary to send a portion of the pork steak and a black pudding to the neighbours, and this was usually reciprocated when their turn came to kill their pig. These customs are now consigned to history as pigs are no longer killed in this manner.

Homebaking was common in most rural households during my youth and my mother made lovely bread, including round loaf and griddle bread. Mam would make a special fire by placing hot coals near the big fire; on this she would put the bastable for the round loaf or the griddle for the griddle bread. During the baking process the coals had to be replenished from the main fire if the temperature was considered to be dropping below the required level, and the bread was twisted or turned occasionally to ensure the loaf was evenly crusted. When fully baked, the loaf was placed on a stand and allowed to cool before being served. Both types of bread were lovely. When she had finished with the losset (a special container for mixing and manipulating the ingredients) Mam would put it to dry and be ready for the next baking.

We had a very good spring well situated at the foot of the fields on the lower part of the farm. The water was crystal clear and was used by many of our neighbours. My father saw to it that is was kept perfectly clean and he would have the water analysed periodically. The well was a favourite spot and a great meeting place when we were growing up and later for making dates! To the left of the last field, by the ditch, was what was known as the *strap an aifreann*, the stile for Mass. My parents told us that it had been used in Penal times by the priest who offered Mass there.

While we were growing up, my parents found it difficult at times to make ends meet. There weren't any grants or subsidies available at that period in Ireland. Six children had to be fed and clothed and, after primary school, secondary education had to be arranged. My only brother, Pa, stayed home after completing primary school to assist my parents on the farm. He was blessed with a great intellect and, while assisting with the work, he always made time for reading, a habit he maintained throughout his life. In addition, he was a man with a great mechanical brain and it was not uncommon to find a television undone on the kitchen table, and by night time it would be put together again and working perfectly.

My parents were aware that they had to be resourceful as money was very scarce. People today may think that recycling is a modern idea, but my mother was already making school satchels for us out of school coats and she remade a lot of our clothes, which were handed down from one to the other. My father kept our shoes and school boots in good repair; with his last, leather, tacks and a sharp knife, he would replace the old soles and heels and make our shoes and boots look like new.

As my sisters Mary Agnes and Eileen grew older they went on to secondary school, while myself, Bridie and Pat continued at primary school. We walked to school daily as did most other children back then. In winter, each household had to supply the school with a few sods of turf to keep the classrooms somewhat warm. I found school difficult, as some teachers were unfriendly and not always kind or understanding. Mr O'Callaghan was an exception. He always called me Maigread beag (little Margaret) and would bypass me when the cane was being used. One lingering memory I have of going to school was seeing my mother stand at the doorway each morning and wave to us until we were completely out of sight: I often longed to be at home with her.

As time moved on, my older sisters finished their education and secured their futures with good jobs. Sheila, the eldest, got a job in an office in Foynes in County Limerick, while Eileen began work with An Post. I was next on the list. In Ireland at that time it seemed only natural that one girl in the family would join the convent and where there were boys, one might go for the priesthood. To have both a nun and a priest in the family was considered to be a great privilege. Indeed, there was an old saying that to have a son a priest was to have a bed in heaven and the nun was an added bonus. In our family, for some reason, it was considered that I would be the one to enter a convent. Mam always thought it, saying that I was quiet, modest and well-behaved.

Nuns frequently visited local schools and encouraged students to consider religious life. At the time, that life appealed to me as I was interested in Africa, but I was too young at twelve or thirteen to make a decision. I continued on with school for the next couple of years but the thought of the convent was in my mind a lot. I thought that my parents favoured the idea and Mam would often start a sentence by saying, "When Madge joins the convent", and she would discuss it with me frequently. My father liked the idea though he did not want to hear about Africa. I knew little about Africa at that time except what I heard from the nuns who visited our school and the descriptions of their lives and work sounded very attractive to me.

In early 1949 my mother and I decided we would make some investigations about convents and where girls were entering. Castleconnell Presentation Convent in County Limerick was the nearest to us with a novitiate. We wrote to the novice mistress, Mother Victoire, who replied immediately suggesting a date for us to visit the convent. On the appointed day my mother and I took a bus to Daly's Cross, near Limerick, and from there we walked the distance to the convent. As we arrived at the entrance we met the caretaker who kindly showed us to the door of the convent. It was a very large building surrounded by a lot of land and beautiful trees, situated near the Shannon River. We rang the doorbell and a lovely young girl, dressed in a black dress and a white veil, opened the door to us and showed us to the sitting room, a beautiful room with lots of polished furniture and a marble fireplace.

Shortly after, Mother Victoire introduced herself and we had a chat while the Sister who had let us in brought a tray of tea and biscuits for us. Mother Victoire gave us all the necessary information and told us that there were about twenty girls in the novitiate at that time. The life she described sounded pleasant to my ears and any nuns I had ever seen always seemed happy, yet I was apprehensive about what might lie ahead. A short time after that initial meeting, Mother Victoire wrote and suggested to my mother that July 16th, 1949, would be a suitable date for me to enter as it was the feast of Our Lady of Mount Carmel. My parents and I agreed to it.

A day never passed that I didn't think about what lay ahead. I had no idea whatsoever about the way nuns lived or what motivated them. I just decided to make the best of the time left to me at home and to enjoy every minute of it. My parents were very aware of my feelings, which were a mixture of excitement and anxiety. I loved home and everything about my life – I loved the countryside, going out with my sisters, being with my parents – and, yet, the thought of Africa and the work I could do there was always in my mind. Because I was entering the convent, I was allowed to leave school for the last few months of the school year. That period in my life was wonderful, as I was at home every day with my parents and my younger sisters.

Occasionally I would help my Dad with the cattle as he had to go to the local fairs and buy new cattle in exchange for the older ones. We did not enjoy the fair days because, when all the bargaining was over and done with, there had to be a celebration in a pub. Dad would walk home and we always knew when he had a few extra pints taken. Mam never liked it and would point out to him all the extra cost of the drink. However, I have a vision of Dad sitting by the fire, with a contrite look on his face, holding the peak of his cap in his hand while looking up at the picture of the Sacred Heart and the little lamp lighting underneath. He would say, "Well, with the help of Jesus and Mary I will never touch drink again". His intentions were very good, anyway, and he was very loving and caring.

In the time before I joined the novitiate, the biggest concession was the fact that I was allowed to attend the local dancehall. I was only fifteen years old but that made no difference. I was terribly excited on the night I made my debut. For years I had heard my sisters and my brother talk about the dancehall and how much they enjoyed themselves there; now I could share that enjoyment and I did. They dressed me up, applied make-up to try to disguise my youth, so much so that nobody was any the wiser. There was always music in the house so we all learned to dance, even the ballroom style, and we had done step dancing in primary school, which cost my parents four pence an evening.

I thoroughly enjoyed my night at the dancehall and attended a number of times. I made friends with a very nice young man, Tommy, who was a few years older than me. At first there was no way I could convince him that I was entering a convent and many questions followed. On my last night out dancing at Athea dancehall, Tommy saw me home and I said goodbye to him at the top of the quarry road. He gave me a kiss, wished me all the best and finally said, "I suppose by this time next week you will be in the convent", and so I was.

The date fixed for my going away was a Saturday and, as it drew closer, I was beginning to have doubts, but soon dismissed them telling myself that I would be happy. My mother had a list of clothes and other items to get for me, and each piece of clothing had to have a nametag attached. The day for my departure from home finally arrived. I dressed up, wearing a lovely red dress and a tweed coat. Mam and Dad and Pa were coming with me, but I had to say goodbye to my two lovely little sisters to whom I was so attached.

A TIME OF SILENCE

Presentation Convent, Castleconnell, County Limerick

1949-1953

We arrived at the convent door and were met by the same Sister who admitted us on the first occasion. We had a short conversation with the novice mistress, Mother Victoire, and then it was time to say goodbye to Mam, Dad and Pa. While they were very lonely leaving me, they were happy in the knowledge that I was in a lovely convent where I would be well-looked after. I said goodbye and saw them off as they drove down the driveway. Heartbroken, I was taken in by the novice mistress and shown to the little chapel where she said an Act of Consecration. She then dressed me in a black habit with a white collar and cuffs and a short, black veil that was known as the postulants' dress. Sister Mary was then given charge of me – each postulant was given what was known as an 'angel'.

There were many dormitories and she took me to St. Joseph's where my cubicle was close to the window and had a good view of the driveway. In the corner of the curtained cubicle stood a stand with a washbasin and jug which were used for daily washing (we had a bath once a week). At suppertime I was taken to the refectory and shown my place at the bottom of a long table. There was a corresponding table at the other side, as well as one across the top for the Superiors. All meals were taken in silence but, on the arrival of a new postulant, we were allowed to talk. In this way I got to know the person next to me. After supper we prayed as we walked up the stairs to the chapel and a short time after that a bell rang for recreation. The Sisters all assembled in the community room where there were two long benches and a chair at the top of the table for the novice mistress.

All the Sisters had some type of work on hand, including knitting, embroidery, making badges for holy pictures, or mending black stockings. We were free to chat away and to get to know each other. At five minutes to nine we were told to tidy up in order to be ready for night prayer. At nine o'clock, a bell would ring – this was to signify the importance of the 'great silence' which could not be broken until after breakfast on the following morning. At the end of night prayer we all walked down the chapel and bowed to the Mother Superior, Mother Theresa, and went quietly to our dormitories. My first night in a convent was full of very different feelings and emotions. Apart from being extremely lonely, I could not understand why there was so much silence and why people only spoke to each other during recreation. Yet, I felt that there must be lots of nice things to come as the Sisters seemed happy and to be enjoying life.

Next morning, a bell rang out good and clear for all to hear. I jumped out of bed and began to dress in my postulant's dress. A Sister arrived at the curtain with the greeting, "Benedicamus Domino", to which one was obliged to reply, "Deo Gratias". Shortly after, my angel arrived to convey me again – and for the last time, as I was now getting familiar with my surroundings – to the chapel. Sisters were doing meditation, which was followed by the Office (the Office was the official prayer of the Church) and was chanted in Latin. How and when was I going to learn all this, I wondered? Mass in Latin followed and a Sister gave all the responses in Latin. It was all so worrying and confusing.

We ate breakfast in silence and with our eyes cast down. Unfortunately for me, on my first day I was given a slice of very fat bacon, so unlike what I was used to from home, and I just couldn't eat it. I couldn't ask the person next to me what I should do with it as we had to observe silence. I looked across the room to discover that the Sisters were progressing with their washing up. I got my square of paper for washing my plate from my drawer in the table which also held a small tea towel for drying up. When I was washing up I dumped the fat meat into the bowel of water but later got into trouble for not eating it. The next task was the completion of individual chores; each Sister was given an assignment for a month as the convent had to be kept perfectly clean. My first chore was dusting the front hall, the staircase and surrounds. That took about an hour, and then the next bell went for the morning lecture.

We all assembled in the community room and sat at the two long benches while Mother Victoire sat at the top of the table. With hands in sleeves and our eyes cast down, we listened to Mother while she read to us from spiritual books. I recall she used to read from one about Fr John Sullivan and Dom Marmion. Occasionally she would test our concentration by asking random questions. Some mornings Mother would sit back in her chair while Sisters acknowledged their faults, including such things as breaking the silence or banging a door. On a more serious level, if one had the misfortune of breaking something such as a cup or dish, that had to be acknowledged in the dining room on one's knees in the presence of the Mother Superior, along with the entire community. She would impose a penance in the form of prayer or the carrying out of a task somewhere in the convent.

We worked outdoors also, as the hens had to be taken care of and while the caretaker took charge of the cows, we took turns looking after the pig. It was a very sad day for a particular Sister who was in charge of the pig when the Mother Superior took a walk down to the garden and found our valuable pig lying stone dead in the yard. The Sister was summoned immediately to the Superior's office and asked to account for the death of the pig. She was asked if she was aware of the importance of the pig to the community. Unfortunately for the Sister, she was unable to give any explanation as when she last saw him he was well and she had fed him. Mother wasn't too happy with her explanation and we were all in sympathy with the Sister.

The convent didn't have a definite income, as the school was not in existence as yet. Money was scarce and the Sisters had bought this large house and farm from a company in Limerick called Shaw's. While the community was partly self-supporting, what with the cows which provided milk from which we made butter, and the hens which provided eggs, we did not enjoy any luxuries except on big feast days when we would have additional food and treats. We also made additional income in springtime when there were lots of lovely daffodils in the garden; we picked them, put them in bunches and they were sold in Limerick. Every few extra pennies helped.

I was still lonely for home; I missed my family desperately but in the convent one could not talk too much about anything. We were always accompanied by the novice mistress and particular friendships were strictly forbidden. The more senior Sisters would see to it that we did not go for walks with the same Sister too frequently. Yet there was one Sister, Sister Josephine, who entered just a few days after I did, and we became very good friends. Sunday nights were the most difficult for me. We went to bed at nine o'clock, and lying there and listening to a band playing in the hall in Castleconnell, which was very close to the convent, was very disturbing. How very different my life had become; recalling the happy nights at home and comparing the two situations made me wonder if I had made a terrible mistake. I wrote home weekly but could not say anything of importance to my parents, or explain how I felt, as mail going out and coming in was censored by the novice mistress. I knew I would not be seeing my parents until after my Reception, that is, if I got that far.

All days were similar, with study, which was difficult for some of us, and recreation twice a day. In the period after lunch we would do some garden work or occasionally go for a walk and that period was much appreciated because you could talk. The convent had a lovely orchard with lots of apple trees, and the apples were delicious. Occasionally we would be sent down to wipe the apples that had been placed on shelves in the loft in the garden shed. We wiped them and replaced them carefully. When the novice mistress was with us we would be given permission to eat one. The apples were frequently served for supper with brown bread and tea, otherwise we would have a slice of cheese. At first, I found working in the garden depressing; just to hear the cars go by and being aware of the rule of enclosure and not being allowed outside the gate, except to go to the doctor or dentist, gave me a terrible feeling of being hemmed in. The second recreation period was at night, just before going to bed, and this period was supervised by the novitiate mistress.

The longing for home and family never left me. I missed my freedom; how I longed to give a run down the fields to the well, which was so much part of our everyday life. Dressing in full black was such a change from the lovely dresses my mother had made for me, but perhaps the future would hold better things for us. I had entered with a view to going to Africa and life would be better there surely, I thought. Because the convent atmosphere had affected me in many ways, I found it almost impossible to say any of my own prayers. Chanting the Office and repeating prayers constantly seemed to have a more artificial feel to it. It was only after Mother Victoire told us the story of the founder of the Presentation Sisters, Nano Nagle, that life began to take on some meaning and gave me an incentive to settle down and grow in her spirit.

Nano Nagle was born into a well-to-do family in Ballygriffin, Mallow, County Cork, in 1718. The eldest of seven children, Nano learned from a young age how to care for and love others. Following her education in France, she returned to Ireland and became the helper of the helpless and founded schools in Cork. Every evening after school she visited the poor, the sick and lonely, and spent herself and her money to help them. When she became short of money she begged for more to continue her work. Nano's immediate work was confined to her native city but her understanding of mission was universal and her motto was, "If I could be of any service in saving souls in any part of the globe, I would willingly do all in my power". Nano founded the congregation of Presentation Sisters on Christmas Eve, 1775. Nine years later on April 26th, 1784, at the age of sixty-six, Nano died in Cork.

The lecture on Nano Nagle from Mother Victoire was inspiring, encouraging and helpful to me as I struggled with doubt, resentment and insecurity. Mother Victoire spoke privately with each of us periodically and she, too, had observed my unhappiness and uncertainty, but she encouraged me to persevere as I was young and assured me that I would gradually settle as I matured. Occasionally, Tommy, my friend of just a few months, occupied my thoughts. He was a lovely person with a gentle and caring personality and I remembered the gentle way he hugged me on that last night and the warmth of his kiss – my first kiss and perhaps my last kiss.

There was a six-month preparation for our Reception ceremony. We were given a rulebook and told to study the contents with a view to living our lives as outlined in the book. The novice mistress observed each one of us as we lived out our lives to the best of our ability, but it was not an easy task to try to live up to the recommended rules. The vows of poverty, chastity and obedience were contained in it among many other subjects. It was recommended to us that if we kept the rule, the rule would keep us. It was also said that we should repeat the phrase, 'Lord, take me, break me and then remake me'. I was just beginning my sixteenth year and I thought it was all most peculiar. One had to be careful, as there was always the possibility of being sent home and that would be terrible for my parents and family. Likewise one couldn't leave for the same reasons. There was a terrible stigma attached to priests and nuns who did leave; I knew of a family where the priest left the priesthood and was not allowed home. I was well aware that would never happen to me, but I would not put the family through the embarrassment.

A retreat had to be undertaken which was directed by a priest who spoke with each of us and tried to give us guidance as he saw fit. Then the community members took a vote and if one got a majority, one was accepted into the community. I was happy to be chosen, as otherwise I would have had to wait for a further six months before becoming a novice. Apart from the spiritual side of the preparations, it was necessary for each of us to be fitted for a new uniform which consisted of a long black dress, black petticoat, black shoes and stockings and a white veil.

My father had always bought our school boots, so he knew our sizes. He bought me a beautiful pair of black shoes for my

Reception, and I was so proud of them. My mother had, on occasion, sent me items such as soap, shoe polish and always a packet of sweets. These, of course, had to be inspected by Mother Victoire. I have a very clear memory of an occasion when she had seen the contents of my package and remarked, "Very nice, Sister, but tomorrow morning I would like you to give away every item contained in this package. Give the contents to the Sisters after the morning lecture". I left her room shattered. Had it been anybody else perhaps I could have accepted the challenge, but I knew how my mother would have scrimped and saved to buy these gifts. How cruel, I thought, but apparently this was in keeping with the vow of poverty.

Harking back to the phrase, 'Lord, take me, break me and then remake me', I wondered if this wasn't part of the breaking, and I also wondered how much more was there to break. Reception preparations continued daily; the bishop was informed along with the local parish priest. Our parents weren't allowed to be present for the ceremony but they would be invited shortly afterward. The Reception ceremony itself was a wonderful occasion. During Mass the choir sang, the bishop gave an encouraging sermon and called us Brides of the Lord. I felt happy and excited and grateful that I had got so far. On my Reception I took the name Aloysius Gonzaga and was known thereafter as Sister Gonzaga.

After our Reception as novices, daily lectures, study, household work and outdoor work continued. We were now expected to give good example to the new, incoming postulants. Knowing how I had felt when I first arrived, my heart went out to them. It was important to smile and at all times to set a good example. During those first months following Reception the household duties varied from month to month. Strangely, none stand out in my mind as vividly as cleaning the bathroom floors. The tiles were black and white and diamond-shaped and I have a complete aversion to black and white tiles ever since! Another vivid memory I have from those early days is of sitting on a windowsill with another novice and looking out the window on the long grass surrounding the convent; we broke silence as I showed that Sister the direction of my home place, the place which never left my heart. She, likewise, showed me the direction of her home and without saying so, I know that she felt as I did.

Another big event was now about to take place and this was the eagerly awaited day when our parents were allowed to visit us. The anticipation was something I cannot describe. My little sister, Pat, had written to me asking me to mention her name in my letters home as the person chosen to visit me with my parents. But without ever mentioning her name, I knew it was understood that Pat would be brought along for the day. She was the baby of the family and we all loved her so very dearly.

On the day of the visit, I was all dressed up in my new habit and white veil and could scarcely wait for the doorbell to ring. My Dad would see my new shoes worn for that special occasion and otherwise kept for Sunday wear. Finally, I heard the doorbell ring; all that was needed was to await the call from the Sister on doorbell duty. She arrived and said my family was in the parlour and went to the kitchen to make them some tea. I went along and gently tapped on the parlour door. But my heart sank when I saw that my little sister was not there. The first words I uttered were, "Where is Pat, why isn't she here?" My Mam and Dad hugged me and, with tears in their eyes and in very soft voices, they explained that Pat was not too well but that she would be fine again soon. That was a huge disappointment; I knew that Pat had often been sick but always recovered and bounced back to her own dear self, so that settled my fears. It was so wonderful so see Mam and Dad again and they were so happy to see me, and now to see me in the nun's habit made them even happier.

The time passed quickly as they had to catch a bus at Daly's Cross at a certain time. When the time to go came, tears flowed copiously as they hugged and kissed me until I finally had to let them go and watch them walk down that long driveway which seemed so endless on that occasion. I was now a nun, so the tears had to be dried quickly and replaced with a smile, but all the time my heart was breaking. I longed for bedtime so that I could cry my heart out. In bed that night I wondered why my parents had tears in their eyes – perhaps it was the emotion of meeting me again and seeing me dressed up in the nun's habit for the very first time? I went asleep with that thought in my mind.

All went well over the following weeks. Each Sister had a visit from her parents and during the night recreation we could discuss the details of each visit. During all this time Mother Victoire was observing our suitability for the religious life. Many things had to be taken into consideration, most importantly, whether we were observing the rule and whether our lives were becoming more spiritual. As Mother would frequently say, "Union with God is most essential". Only prayer and silence could achieve this, and in this respect, I felt I was doing my best. As a young child I always had a great sense of God's presence. The first time I experienced that was one Christmas Day while kneeling before the crib in my own church in Athea. I felt the Lord was close to me and that I was close to Him and that feeling has remained with me all through my life.

March 16th of that year, 1950, is a date which is etched in my mind forever. I was churning milk down in the basement dairy to make butter for the community, when Mother Victoire sent for me. I wondered what I could have done as she usually corrected us where we were working. But on this occasion she conveyed me to my dormitory. She said to sit on the bed and then she told me that she had had a letter from my mother and that my little sister Pat was not well. I asked how sick she was and Mother kept repeating that she was very sick. Again I asked, how very sick is she? Poor Mother Victoire hadn't the heart to say the terrible words and eventually I asked, "Is she dead?" "Yes, she is," she said.

Pat had died on March 11th, five days earlier. Mother wept with me, as it was a horrible task she had to perform, and words will never describe how I felt. Mother went to prayer and I remained on in the dormitory. I recall looking down the driveway and seeing the bare trees that lined it on both sides. I felt numb, away from my family and with nobody to hold my hand or give me a hug. For days and weeks afterwards

I searched my spiritual books, seeking some explanation or consolation, but there was none. My mother, heartbroken and weary, managed to write to me saying that she supposed if God wanted Pat we had to try to be resigned. My father wrote to me to tell me the last words she uttered as he held the crucifix in her little hand. She said, "Dada, don't let me go", but, unfortunately, she had to go.

Life continued and in the midst of our daily life something amazing happened to one of the novices within my group. Despite the high walls and the locked gate and the curtained-off cubicles a lovely relationship developed between one novice, Joan, and a man called Eamon. This relationship later developed into a friendship, which then led to marriage. Mother Victoire was totally unaware of any such occurrence in her novitiate. Some of us who were Joan's close friends and who belonged to her group gradually became aware of what was happening. She was a beautiful looking girl and blessed with long, golden hair which had been cut short at Reception time. Prior to entering the convent Joan was employed by a shop owner in Limerick city. The man concerned, Eamon, was a constant visitor to the convent and proved extremely helpful to the Superiors when they required a car, as they didn't have transport. In this way they were providing him with an opportunity to meet Joan. It transpired that Eamon had always admired Joan and missed her when she entered the convent.

At that time Joan wasn't aware of his feelings for her, but somehow they managed to meet occasionally, and as time went on we were told, but sworn to secrecy. We were faithful to her and assisted them to meet when possible. One occasion stands out in my mind: I was working in the dairy where the butter was churned and made into little pats, which were then put into each Sister's drawer in the dining room for mealtime. Suddenly, to my amazement, I saw Eamon making his way down the embankment and on to the window of the dairy. It was not a window that opened normally but instead had mesh covering it. I wondered how I was going to handle this situation. I spoke with him for a minute and he asked that I call Joan to the window for him. This I did willingly, then left the room to give them an opportunity to chat. The love that they felt for each other was very obvious and showed clearly on their faces.

Another opportunity for meeting arose when Joan was on duty, either in the parlour or on door duty. This love affair continued for some time but the novice mistress was oblivious to the situation, until eventually Eamon decided to speak to Mother Victoire. She was dismayed, shocked, and annoyed with Joan for not telling her when the relationship was at an earlier stage. Joan explained that she didn't know how to say it as she was embarrassed. A short time later, she left and was subsequently married to Eamon in Limerick. Sadly, the other novices were not allowed to wish her goodbye or good luck. We missed Joan terribly and, following her departure, we felt very lonely. Their union was a mystery to the Superiors who made many enquiries as to how this relationship happened. Despite our youth and inexperience, we never revealed that we were aware that anything was taking place. From that day, we never heard about Joan and Eamon, or how life treated them, whether they had a family or whether they continued in business.

A few months after Joan's departure, two more Sisters decided to leave the convent, and they too belonged to our original group of seven. Again the same situation arose – there were no goodbyes; they were just missing from the breakfast table one day, and after the morning lecture Mother Victoire announced in a sad and depressing voice that they had left for good. Naturally, we were lonely and that awful feeling prevailed for many weeks. These departures made me think again and again of my own situation. Where would it all get me? Still, I plodded along and prayed that God would direct me in the right direction because, on my own, I was unable to decide how I should proceed. After a few conversations with the novice mistress and my own simple prayers, I felt I was on the right path, for now anyway.

The next big occasion, our first profession, would not be for another two years when the vows of poverty, chastity and obedience would be taken. Many new faces had come, and some had gone. Our senior Sisters were already professed and had left the novitiate. Luckily we were allowed to say goodbye, not like previous occasions when Sisters left the convent without a word. Study and lectures were still the order of the day. Exams had to be completed, especially the Religious Cert which was necessary for entrance to college. When the time came for first profession, the same procedure took place as at Reception time. The community took a vote as to the suitability of each candidate for continued life in the congregation of the Presentation Sisters. This was a very important occasion as we were now preparing to take vows of poverty, chastity and obedience for one year, and this would be done each year for six consecutive years, and then it was final vows for life.

I managed to pass the various stages and obtained sufficient votes to be admitted to first profession. My parents and I were very happy that I got through. Visitors were not invited for the ceremony which I felt was rather a pity as I would have loved to have seen them, even for a short period, since they knew that I would be leaving the novitiate shortly after profession. The big change that took place during the ceremony was that the white veil was exchanged for a black one. The usual celebrations took place with some lovely meals and lots more time for recreation. On these occasions we were allowed to go for long walks, to cross the little bridge which separated Limerick from Clare. The countryside was just exquisite with the River Shannon flowing gently by and its banks wooded with many beautiful trees. With the trees in such abundance, the birds were equally so, and their early morning song was always uplifting. It was only many years later that I fully appreciated the beauty of Castleconnell and the surrounding area.

The Superiors discussed our destinations and we eagerly awaited their decisions. Eventually I was assigned to Matlock in Derbyshire, England. My companions went to other convents, also in England. While we were happy that we had been successful in our two and a half years' training, we were lonely as we bid each other goodbye and prepared for the next part of our life's journey.

SETTLING INTO RELIGIOUS LIFE

Presentation Convents – Matlock,
Ryde and Penzance, England

1953-1955

I travelled by sea with a small group of Sisters to Holyhead, experiencing a great sense of excitement on seeing the outside world once again and getting to speak with lay people. From Holyhead I travelled on my own to the town of Matlock in Derbyshire. A Sister from Matlock Presentation Convent, who took excellent care of me then and for a long time afterwards, met me on arrival in the town which, for me, was like entering a new world. I was welcomed into a community of around 25 Sisters who ranged in age from the young to the very old, with the majority involved in teaching. There was a large boarding and day school at Matlock where pupils from many parts of England were educated. There were similar schools in many other parts of England run by the Presentation Sisters.

The greater freedom was a welcome experience for me; I welcomed the fact that I could go in to Matlock town, which was within walking distance, accompanied by another Sister. The mere fact of going into shops again was wonderful, if unfamiliar. One of my companions told me that she had once been sent into a shop unaccompanied and very quickly lost her bearings. She was distressed, as a Sister was waiting in the car, so she promptly went to a counter to ask the assistant if, by any chance, she had noticed by which door, she, the Sister, had entered the shop. Another Sister went into a shop in search of a particular garment. She was trying to explain exactly what she required and then she discovered when she wasn't getting a reply that she had been talking to a mannequin! How she hoped that nobody had seen the episode! Many such experiences took place until we became accustomed to living life normally again. I felt very self-conscious initially as this was the first time I was ever out in public in my full habit and I though people on the streets saw us as very different. My self-confidence was at low ebb, but it gradually improved over time.

Matlock Convent had a different atmosphere from that of the novitiate. It took me a few months to settle as I watched the Sisters doing their work, some teaching, while others did the cooking for the community and the boarders, and others still took care of the boarding apartments. I was assigned to work with another Sister in taking charge of the boarders after school hours. At that time it was not difficult to deal with students as they understood supervision from a young age. The terrible loneliness for home became a little easier as I became more involved in the work and I could talk to the Sisters and the students. Matlock wasn't as frugal as the novitiate in

Castleconnell where we had sometimes been hungry, what with post-war food rationing and the general lack of food. Here there was more food available – marmalade was served with breakfast, we got desserts regularly and roast beef and Yorkshire pudding on Sundays, and that was a welcome change.

The fact that I could go down town with another Sister was a huge relief and so different from just listening to the cars go by from inside the walls of the novitiate in Limerick. For a long time I would give a sigh of relief as we walked out the convent gate (we went into town once every five or six weeks); I felt myself breathing in the freedom of the world about me, watching people going about their work in the fields, in the shops and just walking the streets – I thought it was wonderful. Life was coming back to me again and bringing with it a sense of normality.

I settled in at Matlock and although my day-to-day life was relatively uneventful, my thoughts often turned to my unfinished studies and I wondered when I might complete them. Then, sure enough, one evening the Superior took me aside for a little chat. She wondered if I had settled into community life and asked whether I felt happy generally. I assured her I was doing fine and that I liked Matlock. Although she was delighted to hear that, she told me that she was sending me to another convent. As I had no definite job in Matlock, I always knew that I'd be moving on at some stage, but I was very glad to have had the experience of living in community. She then broke the news to me that I would be teaching little boys in a school in Ryde in the Isle of Wight. A Sister had become ill and would be absent from school for some months. The news came as a surprise and I experienced a sense of shock, as I faced a new challenge, a completely new adventure in a new community where I didn't know anyone.

I travelled unaccompanied to Ryde and, fortunately, a Sister Paula, who was the principal of the school at that time, met me at Portsmouth. Sister Paula and I became great friends. She was extremely kind to me and understanding, both of my youth and of the challenge ahead for an eighteen-year-old without any previous teaching experience. She showed me the convent, the school and the classroom I would be using. On the following Monday morning she introduced me to the little five- and six-year-olds, showed me their books and told me to get on with it. After the first week or so I found myself enjoying the teaching and had no problems with the children. I was a bit over-protective at first but then let go and allowed the children be themselves.

During my time there the school inspector visited the whole school and called into my room, accompanied by Sister Paula, who told me later that I had coped quite well and blushed nicely! The five or six months passed very quickly and by that time the Sister whom I replaced had recovered and was now ready to take up her position again. I was sad leaving that convent as I was very happy there and, along with the children and Sister Paula, everything about the community was happy and pleasant. It was a much smaller community than Matlock, consisting of about eight Sisters, so it had been easier to get to know each one personally.

Sister Paula advised the Superiors in Matlock that she thought I should consider training to become a teacher. I was consulted on this but stated that when I decided to enter the convent originally I felt the need to go to Africa and to work as a nurse. Matlock was the headquarters of all the English Presentation Convents at that time and it was there that the Superior General resided, and what she said was law. Her usual approach was to issue instructions through the Superior of the house. I was anxious as to what was to follow when I returned to Matlock but, once I returned, I felt a little more confident and accepted that it was from here that my future would be decided.

After a few days I was once again summoned to the Superior's office. My heart throbbed as I asked myself where and what now? She was delayed a few minutes, but to me it seemed like hours. Eventually she arrived, looking cheerful and happy. I thought this was a good omen. As she sat in her big chair she told me she had got a very good report on my experience in Ryde. The principal was pleased with my work and with my teaching ability with the pupils. She spent some time trying to convince me to train for teaching. I asked for a little time to consider both nursing and teaching.

I was very much aware of how enjoyable my time in Ryde had been. I had enjoyed walking through the lovely town of Ryde and the Sisters had taken me to see many places of interest. I loved the countryside with its many different fields, the cattle grazing, the sheep eking out a living from the hedges. It had reminded me of home, and home and my family were never too far from my thoughts. After a few days and having prayed a good deal, I made my desire to train as a nurse known to the Superior. She was a person of great understanding and explained to me that I would have to complete my education to obtain my A Levels before anything definite could be decided.

I took up my student supervision duties once again at Matlock and occasionally took trays to sick or elderly Sisters. I would offer to make their beds and see that the room was clean. At last I felt I was doing worthwhile work – looking after the sick was a joy for me, I felt extremely happy when I had made them comfortable and left them with a smile on their faces. Yes, I thought, this seems to be the way forward for my future. Teaching was marvellous also, but somehow I didn't feel the same way about it. This experience at Matlock gave me the determination which I had when I first decided to enter the convent. The sick and, in particular, the sick in Africa, were my priority.

A few weeks later I got another message that the Superior wanted to speak with me. It was always a bit nerve-wracking, wondering what was about to take place. I didn't have too long to think as she was waiting in her office and when she greeted me with a smile I knew immediately that I wasn't in any kind of trouble. The subject the Superior wanted to discuss with me was the completion of my studies. The place chosen for me to do this was Penzance in Cornwall. I had heard of Penzance and Mother explained that the community there had amalgamated with the Matlock group a few years previously. It was a happy feeling to know that I would be doing my studies finally but, in another way, I was sad at leaving Matlock, as I had been equally so at leaving Ryde, where I had an experience I would never forget and where the kindness of Sister Paula was an example for me for the rest of my life.

In a few days I had my bags packed once more. Mother Superior conveyed me to the train and explained what changes I would have to make en route. I recall that it was an extremely long journey and, being alone, I found it all the longer. My thoughts kept going back to Matlock and Ryde, and I hoped I would be as happy in Penzance as I had been in these two convents. It was night time when I arrived at the railway station in Penzance and at this stage I was tired, hungry and very apprehensive. However, I got a very warm welcome at reception from Mother Dympna, who was the Superior and a lovely person. She was aware of the long journey I had undertaken so she ordered the Sister in the kitchen to prepare a meal for me, and after that she sent me to bed. Next day I was introduced to each of the Sisters, all of whom were kind and welcoming. On the following day I was taken by some of the Sisters to view Penzance and the surrounding area with its lush farmland, and I thought it lovely.

The decision to send me to Penzance was to help me study for the A Level exams but, by now, I was out of the habit of doing real study. The principal of the secondary school, Sister Mary, thought I should attend class with the other A Level students, and Sister Philomena offered to give me private tuition in the evenings. I was delighted with these arrangements and I started studying almost straight away. At first it was difficult as the other students were well ahead of me but, with the private tuition, I was managing to cope quite well.

The Penzance community were kind and very hard-working. They visited the sick all over the parish and seemed to live their lives very much in accordance with the principles of Nano Nagle. A couple of Sisters had taken on caring for the sick and elderly in the parish while another looked after the sick in the hospital, and others took care of the parish church. The community was less in number (six in total) than Matlock or Ryde, but their all-round commitment was very inclusive. For recreation at weekends we took long walks, playing tennis occasionally, and at night we played scrabble and other games. I was treated to trips, visiting Truro, Land's End and many other places of interest.

Life continued happily for about six months and I knew that my schoolwork was improving. I felt that I would be ready to take the A Level exams when the time came. But, as the phrase says, 'man proposes and God disposes', and this was very true in my case. Completely out of the blue, a tall, erect nun arrived at the convent in Penzance. She was one of the Presentation Sisters who had left India after it gained Independence, and she was the first Superior to take charge of the Sisters in Rhodesia (now Zimbabwe) in Africa. During her visit to Penzance she asked to see me and informed me that she had heard that I had expressed a desire to go to Africa. I told her that was true, and added that just now I was busy preparing to do my exams. She immediately replied that I could continue my studies in Africa.

It transpired that she, Mother Bernard, and another Sister, Mother Peter, were home on holiday from Africa and were recruiting volunteers. Mother Bernard thought it would be a good idea if I went with them. I didn't really have a choice and, had I been given one, I would have finished my studies, where I was so happy and doing so well. But I had taken a vow of obedience and so had to submit to the will of my Superiors. Mother Bernard told me she would speak with me again in a few days' time. In the meantime, I prayed that she would change her mind, but the opposite was the reality.

It was decided that I would travel to Africa with Mother Bernard and Mother Peter one month later when they were returning to Rhodesia. Mother Bernard had everything under control and I was sent straight away to get vaccinated against tropical diseases. There was one good thing to come from this decision – I was to be allowed home to see my family for ten days' holiday before leaving for Africa. I was completely overjoyed at the thought of going in the door at home, meeting my parents and family, and walking again through the fields I knew so well. At the same time, I was getting excited at the thought of going to Africa. At night I could scarcely sleep, thinking about it all.

But a huge shock was to follow; on one of the days of preparation while Mother Bernard was with us, she called me aside and, while talking about my home holiday, she casually informed me that I would not be allowed home again for twenty years. I was completely shocked and almost dropped at her feet. I asked myself how she could say that to me on the eve of my holiday. Could she not wait, I wondered, until I had had my holiday and we were on the boat to Africa, where she would have ample time to break the news. I reckoned that Mother Victoire in Limerick would never have done that to me; she had treated me so gently and lovingly when my sister died.

I worried about what my parents would be like after another twenty years. Many questions were going through my mind and I found it very difficult to accept the twenty-year barrier. All the different ups and downs of the novitiate were so trivial compared to this, but that was the situation and I just had to try to accept it. Perhaps Mother didn't think it was going to be so hurtful and so painful for me, but it was. Neither did it help me to know that she would be our Superior during the long haul out to Rhodesia and for many years to follow. I spoke in confidence with one of the Sisters in Penzance and she helped me greatly. She had had very difficult experiences also, but managed to overcome them all in time. She advised me that things would get better for me also, and said that while life itself can be tough, God is there for us at all times, only to trust in Him. I took courage and consolation from what she said but I decided not to tell anybody about the twenty-year absence from home as it was far too painful to admit, even to myself.

A date in October of that year, 1955, was decided on which I would leave Penzance to travel to Ireland for my holiday. I said my farewells with a sad heart in one sense, but I was greatly excited about going home. The Sisters were so understanding and so kind, especially my tutors, who regretted that I hadn't gotten the opportunity to complete the course. A few of them saw me off at the station in Penzance; they sent their very best wishes with me and a promise of prayers as well. From Penzance I took a train to Bristol and there I changed trains and boarded one to Fishguard. I was feeling very tired when I got on the boat to Rosslare. For the last lap of the journey I took a train to Limerick, where I knew that my Mam and Dad would be waiting for me. Watching out the window of the train, my neck was strained from waiting for a sighting of them.

Eventually the train stopped at Limerick station and there they were, all excited, and the hugging and kissing was wonderful. They were so delighted to have me to themselves again. This was the first time in years that we could speak on our own. We went for lunch, but I was so excited I had no interest in food. We soon set out for home and I thought how wonderful it would be for me just to go in the door of the house again. Unfortunately, there was a huge gap in our home since I was last there - the absence of my little sister, Pat. I was shown the bed where she lay when she uttered her last words, "Dada, don't let me go". I asked to sleep in her bed that night and I occupied it for the remainder of my holiday. I can honestly say that it helped me a lot, and I felt much closer to her and believed that she would help me all through my life, and she did.

The moment I walked in home I caught sight of my mother's lovely round loaves of bread, and there was that lovely homely smell of fresh baking and cooking. In addition, the house was spotless; I imagined the painting and white-washing that had taken place. The hedges in front of the house were all neatly trimmed and tidy, and all for me. Waking up in the morning without bells ringing and racing to get duties done on time was just heavenly. After my experience of living in large convents I felt that the house was very small, but that was to be expected. While my Mam prepared breakfast, I got my longed-for wish to give a run to the well. It was such a joy to see the fields and the cattle, and to breathe the fresh air once again. Surely, I thought, there is no place on earth like home and the family left nothing undone to make my holiday enjoyable.

My Dad whisked up a fresh egg each morning and added milk and sherry to it. Before lunch he opened a bottle of beer, poured out half a glass, and to that he added milk and a couple of spoons of sugar. It was lovely and I looked forward to that drink every day. He maintained always that it was very good for the health, and would give it to us when we were sick. Dad went to town daily to bring home goodies for me, but with all the excitement, I found it difficult to eat, especially for the first few days. My parents were anxious to take me to visit different places, but I wasn't interested in any place but home.

Many neighbours, friends and former school companions called and I enjoyed seeing them all. The days were going by terribly fast and, naturally, I wanted my holiday to go on and on but, as the saying goes, 'all good things come to an end'. Just two days now remained of my memorable holiday. I heard the family talk about a farewell party but I didn't like the idea as I felt that it would make me even more lonely. But I didn't say anything and it turned out to be a wonderful occasion. On the

morning of the day before my departure, I was shocked when
a barrel of beer arrived at the house. My brother Pa and a very
good friend and neighbour of ours, Billy Histon (a man that
practically lived in our house, and a person to whom we were
all attached when we were growing up), were responsible for
the organisation of the party and nothing was left undone.

News spread around the locality, and by early evening the
house was full of neighbours and friends. Music of all kinds
rang out and soon we were all out dancing, bringing back
memories of earlier times. With old and new songs and stories
of times past, the hours passed all too fast. Food of all kinds was
in abundance and it was obvious that everybody was enjoying
an extraordinary night as we relaxed and made the night one
that would not be forgotten for many a long day.

At some point during the party, I gave a glance at the clock
to discover that I would be leaving home in just a few hours. My
mother insisted on sending me to bed to get some sleep before
departing. Finally, all was quiet, and the family was able to down
a cup of tea before the painful goodbyes took place. My Mam,
Dad and Pa were taking me to Castleconnell. I was simply heartbroken and I wondered when, or if, I would ever see my family
again. But I remembered the words of the Sister in Penzance
who had told me that God would help me through it, and He
did. On the journey I was silent, as the thought of the twenty-
year ban on returning to Ireland and the fact that I could not tell
my family about it, hung like a shadow over me.

When we reached the convent in Castleconnell, Mother
Victoire was there and I was happy to see her. I discovered that

I would be travelling to London with a beautiful Sister called Mother Theresa, who was the essence of kindness, sympathy, love and compassion. She took the time to explain the route we would be taking to Rhodesia to my parents and Pa. They were happy to know, especially Pa, who would be able to trace the entire route.

Once again, it was time for goodbye, and I saw them off and waved them out of sight. I wondered what they would be like when, or if, I saw them again. I was so glad that Pa was there to give them support. Although I was brokenhearted, I never doubted that I was doing the right thing. Mother Theresa had experienced much of what I was enduring at this time, and so she felt for me and did everything possible to help me. She allowed my tears to flow and encouraged me to rest as there was a very long journey before me. She suggested that we give ten minutes to Our Lady and say the Rosary; I have never forgotten the comfort I got from that prayer at that trying time.

SAILING TO AFRICA

November 1955

Mother Theresa and I travelled to London where we met up again with Mother Bernard, Mother Peter and another young nun, Sister Francesca. I said goodbye to my lovely travelling companion and sadly never saw her again. Mother Peter was returning to Africa after a holiday home in Ireland. She hadn't been home for about twenty years and, unfortunately, her mother died just before she arrived in Ireland. She, too, was very lonely and upset but, despite all that, she was wonderfully kind to us. Everything was new to Sister Francesca and me, and Mother Peter showed us great kindness and understanding. We boarded a train in London which took us to Dover from where we crossed to Calais. I recall it was a turbulent journey and I felt quite ill, but thankfully only for a short period.

We were bound for Venice and I was excited to see the beauty of that city as I had read a lot about it. Prior arrangements had been made by the Superiors that we could spend a few days there while waiting for the boat. However, the great beauty of Venice was lost on me because the keen loneliness I was feeling

On the family farm in Direen, Athea, Co Limerick, 1947.
L-r: Mary Agnes (sister), Margaret (author),
Sarah (mother), Sheila and Pat (sisters).

Outside Presentation Convent, Castleconnell, Co Limerick,
after Margaret's Reception into the Order in 1950.
L-r: Pa (brother), Sarah (mother), Margaret (author), Paddy (father).

*Paddy (father) and Margaret (author) on the grounds of
Presentation Convent, Castleconnell, Co Limerick, 1950,
following Margaret's Reception into the Order.*

*Sarah and Paddy Ahern, at home in Direen,
Athea, Co Limerick, in the late 1950s.*

Margaret pictured at her final profession at St Michael's Covent,
Borrowdale, Rhodesia (Zimbabwe) in 1956.

*Margaret with friends in the grounds of
Mount Melleray Mission in the early-mid 1970s.*

*Margaret with a child at an outlying clinic in
Rhodesia (Zimbabwe) in the mid 1970s.*

seemed to blur the beauty of the place. I recall visiting a few sites of interest to tourists, including St. Mark's Cathedral and the famous glass factory, as well as watching the gondolas. We stayed in a convent that was owned by French Sisters who were very accommodating and kind despite our language differences.

Soon the ship, the *MV Africa*, was ready to go to sea. We thanked the Sisters for having us and for their hospitality and, stepping on the boat, we looked back and waved, but there was nobody to cheer us on our way. Now we were truly gone from home and homeland. Mother Bernard informed us that we would be sailing for 19 days and 19 nights and on arriving in Beira in East Africa, we would travel by train for a further three days and nights, and would eventually arrive in Rhodesia (now Zimbabwe) in the town of Salisbury (now Harare).

My immediate impressions on the boat were of the smells – I could smell fish, sea water and food. I have a very keen sense of smell at the best of times and then I found the smells overpowering and constant. When we eventually set sail and went on deck I settled and no longer felt overwhelmed by various smells. Mother Bernard and Mother Peter occupied the top bunks while Sister Francesca and I were given the lower bunks. Sister Francesca was a charming travelling companion. No doubt, she too felt lonely having left home and family. She was a few years older than me (I was twenty when I undertook that first trip), and she was lucky, because she had completed her teacher training.

Being on the *MV Africa* was an awesome experience and for the first few days the sea was relatively calm, thank God. This gave us an opportunity to focus our minds on what was happening and what was going to happen. We were aware that communication with other passengers was not allowed, so it was somewhat like being in the novitiate except for the constant sound of the waves hitting off the sides of the boat. Mother Bernard gave us spiritual books to read, but newspapers, magazines and novels were forbidden. She encouraged us to do embroidery and knitting. Unfortunately for us, it was November, and the warmest time of the year and, like all Sisters, we were dressed in full black, including a black habit, black petticoat, black shoes and stockings, and a black veil. It was very hot so we had to make sure and stay in the shade where possible.

There were a number of priests on board, which meant we could avail of daily Mass. Mother would call us early for morning prayer, daily Office and Mass. Without the assistance of these, and my own prayer life, I don't think I could have survived this testing time. Sister Francesca was wonderful, she had a great sense of humour and she could laugh and see the funny side of difficult situations. The boat was Italian, so the food was mainly Italian and while it was new to us, I enjoyed it, as it was different with many unusual flavours.

Meal times were funny occasionally. It so happened that the priests on board managed to seat themselves directly across from Sister Francesca and myself. They seemed to be fully aware of our situation where silence was of the essence and they used every occasion possible to make us laugh, and that was not difficult. When fruit was served at table they would start throwing the apples or oranges over their shoulders and into the cowl at the back of the habit. They would then give a big laugh and it was impossible for us not to laugh. Mother had her back to them so she was unaware of what was happening and wondered what on earth we could be laughing at. I would have loved to chat with them but that was not allowed.

Day followed day with much the same routine and going on deck was somewhat of a relief, especially with Mother Peter, who told us so much about Africa and Rhodesia. Mother had spent many years in India where she took her training and midwifery. Even though she was lonely herself on this trip she always tried to keep the bright side out for our sakes. I found it difficult seeing young couples on deck enjoying themselves; some would sit on the benches close to one another where they would acknowledge their love for each other by hugging and kissing, chatting, laughing, and occasionally enjoying a drink or a glass of wine. Perfectly normal I thought to myself, and had I stayed out of the convent I presume I would be doing likewise. But I had chosen a very different way of life; I had taken vows of poverty, chastity and obedience, which saw life in a very different light, one that we had to be sheltered from at all times.

As our journey progressed, we eagerly looked forward to going ashore at some ports. Port Said in Egypt was our first port of call. How lovely it was to step on land again in a place we had scarcely heard of, and one that I never saw again. The Arabic traders we met and spoke with were polite, but Mother held the purse strings and so we did not have money to buy anything. The last time I had had money was on my journey from Cornwall to Ireland and on my arrival home I had two shillings left over. At Port Said, Mother purchased items of interest and things that would be helpful to her at Christmas time as gifts for people such as the bishop and others. The next stop was Dar es Salaam in Tanzania. We sailed on from there and as we did, the weather was getting warmer all the time. Mogadishu was the next port and then Mombasa, where we disembarked.

Irish Holy Ghost priests lived and worked in this area and they were a joy to meet. Mother had told us that we would be going to confession when we arrived in Mombasa and she very quickly had it all arranged. The priest sat under a tree in the coolest possible place and he kindly cleansed us of all our inequities. After this we were invited to tea – what a joy to taste what seemed liked good Irish tea and refreshments. There were three priests on that mission and to my great joy I discovered that one, Fr O'Neill, was from Abbeyfeale, a town near to where I grew up.

He told me that I must have at some stage eaten O'Neill's bread, which came from Abbeyfeale. To find someone from so near home was a great surprise and a very pleasant one. Mother invited the priests to dinner on the boat that night and later they drove us all around the sea front. Mombasa was a beautiful place and a foretaste of what was to come in Rhodesia. We bade them farewell as we set out on the last lap of the sea trip. Before leaving, Fr O'Neill said he hoped I wouldn't lose my lovely rosy cheeks. Mother replied, saying that I would "just like all the others had done".

Back on the boat, both Mother Peter and Sister Francesca were suffering from heat exhaustion and they were ill for a day or two following our day trip through the beautiful city of

Mombasa. At this stage of our journey, we were accustomed to the large waves, I was constantly saying to myself "water, water everywhere", as there was nothing else in sight but waves and more waves. Occasionally at night when the very strong waves seemed to shake the boat, I would feel nervous and longed for the day we would put foot on *terra firma* again. The port of Beira in Portuguese East Africa was the final stop on the sea journey. While it was a relief to reach land and get out of the boat, Beira was simply roasting hot. Mother Bernard knew some people there who kindly took care of us until it was time to take the slow train to Salisbury. Late in the evening we said farewell to our friends and got to our train.

As was the situation on the boat, we were assigned bunks as it was a three-day and night trip. My bunk was black with beetles and other insects that had come in from the sea. That, combined with the heat, was anything but pleasant. I shed a few tears, much to the horror and disgust of Mother Bernard who said, "Fancy a young Sister crying over a few beetles". I thought the situation deserved a few tears! On we went through the lovely country of Mozambique. I just loved it as it was rugged, mountainous and so colourful. Mother Peter had told us that Rhodesia was equally beautiful and I was so happy to hear that because, in some sort of way, the lovely countryside reminded me of parts of Ireland, although the trees and shrubs were completely different to those at home.

On we went, slowly but surely, and everything was lovely until the mosquitoes began to bite. I'm convinced that they knew that I was only 20 years of age and they surely had a feast! My first bath was spent scratching from head to toe. Was it young blood they enjoyed, I wondered? Sister Francesca was also bitten but not to the same extent. Some mornings I would appear with lumps on my eyes and every place. Of course, we had all taken anti-prolactive treatment for tropical diseases and we had mosquito nets covering our beds, but I thought they would leave me without a drop of blood! Mother supplied us with repellents and cream and we survived, but the mosquitoes continued to be very fond of my blood.

However, in spite of all the discomfort, I slept well on the rickety train and the food was lovely and, somehow, Sister Francesca and I had many a good laugh. She was keen on birds and was constantly on the lookout for African birds. The only animals we saw en route were baboons and we were fascinated to see them run in and out of the rocks, carrying their young on their backs. Mother said we would probably hear hyenas at night – I didn't but I think I was too busy fighting with the mosquitoes!

The days on the train seemed long, no doubt because of my great anticipation at finally seeing Rhodesia, as well as the thought of having a warm bath and a proper bed to sleep in once again. During this time Sister Francesca and I learned a lot from Mothers Bernard and Peter about how the Presentation Sisters had come to Rhodesia from India. When India obtained its Independence the Indian Sisters were ready to take over from the missionary nuns of many congregations including the Presentation Sisters. Both Mothers Peter and Bernard had qualified in India, where Mother Peter studied nursing and midwifery, and where Mother Bernard studied teaching.

Mother Peter explained that, during the mid to late 1940s, discussions about the Presentation Order undertaking missionary work in Africa took place. Mother Josephine O'Connor was the Superior General during all those years of negotiations and it was finally decided that the Sisters' next calling would indeed be to form missions in Africa. The vicar apostolic of Salisbury was Doctor Aston Chichester, a Jesuit, and he was in communication with the Presentations Sisters for some time. He was anxious to find a congregation of Sisters who would take up work in his vicariate. Bishop Donal Lamont, who was a Carmelite from Ireland, was equally anxious to get Sisters for his diocese.

Finally, and after much discussion, it was at Bishop Lamont's diocese that the Sisters decided to take up work (at a later date work was undertaken in Bishop Chichester's diocese also). Finally, the group of pioneers was chosen for Africa and they included Mother Bernard Ryan (the great-great-granddaughter of David Livingstone, great missionary and explorer of Central Africa), Mother Peter, Sister Marie Louise, Sister Benignus and Sister De Lourdes. In 1949, the party left Madras for Bombay, from where they sailed to Mombasa, arriving on African soil on April 29th. They called at Zanzibar and Dar es Salaam and eventually arrived in Beira, from where they travelled to Umtali (now Mutare), where they were warmly welcomed and told that the mission they were going to was called Mount Melleray.

Mount Melleray Mission was in the countryside, about one hundred miles from Umtali, and the journey there was very rough. The roads were mere dirt tracks with huge dips and you had to cross riverbeds en route. Mother Peter told us that while on that awful journey she kept thinking that no matter what hardships she had to face, she could manage provided they had a bathroom and toilet at Mount Melleray – they had neither. In fact, life was quite difficult there at that time; bread had to be made from hops, and meat was available only when the priests or Brothers went hunting. Occasionally they would arrive back with wild pig or kudu or some other game. Sufficient water was a also big problem, but a stream flowed nearby and that was a great help.

The mission at Mount Melleray was originally set up by German Dominican Sisters and German priests and Brothers. They established a school and a small, basic hospital which consisted of two thatched huts. Mother told us lots of stories and one in particular impressed us greatly. One night a man made his way to the hospital and Mother Peter went to his attention immediately, to discover that he had infant twins in a suitcase. He had travelled for hours across mountains and streams. The following day the mother of the twins arrived, and to her great joy both infants had survived the journey and Mother Peter had them wrapped up and nice and cosy in a makeshift basket. Such stories inspired me to stay true to my desire to be of service to people as a nurse.

NEW BEGINNINGS

St Michael's Convent, Borrowdale, Rhodesia

1955-1971

As we neared our destination, Sister Francesca and I were getting excited and looking forward to meeting the Sisters, some of whom we knew. The train began to get slower and eventually drew to a stop at Salisbury railway station. The first person to arrive on the platform was Fr Erdozain, a tall, grey-haired priest dressed in grey. Mother Bernard had told us about Fr Erdozain, whom she knew very well, on the train journey. He was chaplain at St. Michael's school, which was our final destination and where I would be living initially. He would be saying Mass daily in the convent chapel, she explained, and he would hear the Sisters' confessions and would be a general advisor to Mother. After the introductions we moved on quickly to meet the Sisters. That was just wonderful – the welcome, the excitement and the joy at our arrival were indeed memorable.

With the luggage taken care of, we got into a large motorcar and an African man who was the driver closed the door. His name was Rodger and he became a very good friend of mine later on. We were now on our way to St Michael's Convent, which was about nine miles from Salisbury and situated in the countryside. It had been built under the guidance and hard work of Mother Bernard while she was endeavouring to teach and cope with running Mount Melleray Mission station at the same time. We were absolutely overawed by the natural beauty of Salisbury and the surrounding countryside. The sky was brilliant blue and cloudless; it was November and the jacaranda trees, which had been in full bloom, were now shedding their leaves and forming what looked like a carpet all along the streets and pavements. The brilliant red poinsettia was a sight to behold and there was bougainvillea everywhere.

When we arrived at St Michael's Convent the *céad mile fáilte* that awaited us was one that I could never forget. The Sisters were so delighted to see us and we immediately felt at home. Mothers Bernard and Peter were extremely tired and after a delightful, home-cooked Rhodesian meal, they retired for the night. I was not tired, as I was far too excited and there was so much to talk about, with stories galore on both sides. Most of the Sisters had come to Salisbury by plane, so their experiences were less spectacular than St Francesca's and mine, but they too had their own eventful moments which they were willing to share.

We were taken on a tour of the convent which was originally a small bungalow and the Sisters had made many changes to convert it into a convent. There was a dining room and the chapel, which was very neatly arranged, had a verandah overlooking a lovely view of the grounds and the driveway. There were two dormitories, with accommodation for four Sisters in each, while the two Superiors had their own rooms. Because it was such a small building, and so unlike all the other large convents I had lived in, I felt it had a more homely atmosphere which delighted me.

The convent was on the same grounds as St Michael's preparatory school, which was a large school for young boys, including boarders and day-pupils, ranging in age from five up to eleven years of age. Many of the pupils came long distances from such places as Northern Rhodesia, Nyasaland and Matabeleland. The day-pupils came from the local area, and they were the lucky ones, as many of those who came from afar were lonely, missing their parents and families. All of the students were the children of white parents; no African children were allowed attend St Michael's at the time I arrived there.

A swimming pool was central to the lives of the students; in addition they enjoyed tennis, cricket, football and swings, and the younger boys enjoyed slides. Their accommodation in the dormitories was well-planned with plenty of fresh air and they enjoyed good food at all times. While taking a walk in the grounds, the first tree that caught my eye was a large jacaranda just outside the convent's kitchen door – it was huge and laden with blooms. The grounds were very interesting and manicured to perfection, and the driveway was lined with bohemia trees, which were a delicate pale pink and white colour.

Having seen the convent and the grounds of what was to be our home for the foreseeable future, it was decided we would retire for the night. A proper bed without beetles, bugs and, hopefully, without mosquitoes, was a most welcome change. Next morning I woke up late, having had a pleasant, undisturbed sleep. The Sisters were wearing white as it was the hot season (they changed into black for the remainder of the year). After a couple of days I began to feel acclimatised and to settle in at St. Michael's. Mother Peter returned to her mission at Mount Melleray; she loved her work there and promised she would tell us more history and stories about India when we went there on holiday. I longed to see that place and it was a place that became very close to my heart some years later. Mother Bernard remained on at St. Michael's until her retirement many years later. She was a very good person but her nature and personality were distant, strict and lacking in trust.

Once again, silence was enforced except at recreation time. From my first day in the novitiate I disliked and resented the silence. I didn't mind the great silence at night as I could see some meaning to it, but otherwise I felt it was silence for silence sake and it didn't do anything for me. Above all, we were forbidden to speak to priests and secular people, which must have been difficult for the Sisters in school. On one occasion I was serving breakfast to a priest in the parlour. He was telling me about his mother going to Lourdes and I found I could not get him to stop talking, but neither could I just walk out. A few minutes later there was a knock on the door and Mother popped her head in to tell me that she hadn't sent me in to entertain. Both the priest and I felt very embarrassed. Some months later the same priest arrived in again from a mission. This occasion was a special feast day so the nice priest gave me a box of chocolates. I was terrified that Mother would appear again, so this time we cut our conversation short and, on leaving, he said, "Whatever you do, don't declare the chocolates!"

I settled into life at St Michael's and was given duties similar to those I had performed in Matlock, looking after the boarding school and supervising the boarders with Sisters Stanislaus and Ursula. Life in St Michael's was very strict. Both Mothers Bernard and Oliver were all over the place and, as the convent was small, it was not easy to avoid them. One Sister, however, gave us great enjoyment; Sister Mary taught the junior class and occasionally after school we would gather in her classroom, which was away from the big school, and she would entertain with songs and music for an hour. Sister Mary had an outstanding singing voice and I have never heard a rendition of 'Danny Boy' as good as hers. We were allowed to use the amenities available to the students. Swimming was relaxing and most of us enjoyed tennis. On feast days we would have a whist drive. We were also lucky that we owned our own projector and were able to get films at a very reasonable price from a shop in Salisbury. All films, of course, had to be suitable for children, but in those days there were lovely films and two of my favourites were *The Great Waltz* and *Love Story*.

Books, magazines and papers were strictly forbidden, but somehow we managed at times to lay our hands on a book. The only way to read was to get washed quickly at night and have a read in bed, and then hide the book under the mattress. One memorable occasion for me was when I got a nice book in the children's library. It was my duty to supervise the students while they did their study, and all classrooms had large, long windows so one always had a view of who was coming from the convent. On this particular evening I was engrossed in my book and forgot to glance across at the convent. Soon a step arrived on the rostrum beside me and the headmistress, Mother Oliver, said, "What is it you are reading, may I ask, Sister?" "A book about silence, Mother," was my smart reply. She took up the book and announced its proper title, *The Silence of the Hills*, hardly a book on silence. In disgust she put it in her black apron pocket saying, "I shall see Mother about this", and she did. I didn't get to read the end of the story but I would say Mother Oliver did, as I know that she read late into the night. I think she would have enjoyed it because I loved what I had read of it.

St Michael's was wonderful from the view point of the delightful colourful surroundings and the amenities, but it differed greatly from Matlock and Penzance. The atmosphere was tense and I got the feeling of not being trusted. Without trust in human beings I feel that life becomes unbearable. With trust we find peace, joy and love, and trusting in people often helps to relieve us of some of our burdens. Not being allowed to talk to lay people or to priests made life much more difficult. If one met a priest and had a few simple words of greeting with him, just sufficient to be polite, one was expected to report it to Mother. I clearly recall being in the grounds one day and greeting a religious Brother who happened to be on one side of the hedge I was walking by. He was a very old gentleman and I'm sure he was as anxious to get away from me as I was to get away from him. A few hours later I was sent for and told to give an explanation for this long conversation. I was dumbfounded and did not reply. Mother said, "I'm waiting for a reply" and I simply said, "I have none".

The chaplain, Fr Erdozain, did his duty perfectly in every way; total dedication to his work was his motto. In my heart of hearts I had formed my own opinion of this great Jesuit on my first meeting with him, and I didn't change my opinion over time. In some respects he was like Mother Bernard herself. He wasn't as strict as his appearance portrayed, but yet he wasn't keen on seeing us wander too far from the convent. There was a small town close to the convent called Borrowdale and there was a shortcut to the town from the grounds. Frequently after school we would go for a walk and invariably we would just go for a walk down the shortcut without going into the town. Fr Erdozain must have heard or seen us because he later asked Mother, "What is the attraction down Borrowdale road?" We were upset, as we were adults and now we had nothing left for our walks but the stretch from the driveway down to the gate.

At no stage was there a mention of my studies, which had been promised before I left the convent in Penzance. Soon, I feared, I would be out of the habit of doing study and would, perhaps, have forgotten what I had already done. Salisbury University was just across the road from the convent and was ideal for Sisters who were capable of doing further studies, but it was not to be. Fear created a lot of nervousness in our lives; I found proof of this on occasion when we were reciting the Office, the official prayer of the day. During the Office psalms were recited and two Sisters would have to go to the middle of the floor. Firstly we would bow to Mother and ask her blessing in Latin. As soon as we started to chant on our own I would get a fit of giggling and so would the other Sister. Just nothing could stop us and we would resume our places without having completed the psalm. This annoyed Mother intensely and she would deal with us afterwards. It didn't do any good as we were just as bad on the next occasion. I often prayed that the phone would ring or something would happen to occupy Mother for those few moments and we wouldn't laugh at all then.

During this time and throughout my time in Rhodesia we were restricted to two airmail forms per month for letter writing. On big feast days, such as Christmas and Easter, we would be given an extra two forms. All letters going out and coming in were censored and this rule prevailed in all congregations. The family at home was blissfully unaware of my true situation. Mother read each letter thoroughly – this was obvious from remarks passed indicating she had read them. It was difficult enough knowing that they were being read, but to walk into the room while she was reading one's letter was more hurtful. A Sister told me that a situation once arose when she desperately wanted to write to a priest friend of hers without having her letter read, so she thought of a plan. We were well aware of the time the post was taken out and that a long, coarse bag hung inside the door of Mother's room where she would put the letters. Sister Susanna watched for her chance. When she saw Mother put in the letters and leave the room, Susanna took out her envelope, carefully opened it, took out the letter and put in her private letter. She stuck the envelope very carefully and at least she got her wish.

Many years prior to that, Sister Aloysius was teaching at an outside station, and during the course of her work she had a certain amount of contact with the priest in charge. The priest went home on holiday as was the norm. Sister decided she would write to him to let him know how life on the mission was. Knowing Sister Aloysius as we all did, we would not be surprised at any remark she would pass, as she was full of fun and jokes. In her letter she called Father 'honey bunch', a not uncommon term for her to use. However, she was most unfortunate as her letter was returned to her mission and fell into the hands of the new priest in charge. He was one of the curious ones and decided to read it. When he saw 'honey bunch' he put his own connotation on it and decided to send the letter to Mother Bernard. We heard later that he was asked by one of his kinder companions why he didn't send it to the Pope while he was at it! Mother Bernard, in a shocked state, summoned poor old Aloysius. Her council were also called for the meeting and only for the charity and pure common sense of two of the Sisters, I'm not sure what the outcome for Sister Aloysisus would have been.

School holidays were coming and we knew we would be allowed out to the rural areas where all the mission stations were situated. Sister Francesca and myself were informed we would be going to Avila, a mission station about 50 miles from St Michael's. This mission was in a low altitude and it was very hot there, with little or no water, but we didn't mind once we were free and we could converse with people. Of course, we hadn't a word of the local language but the priests were very kind to us and took us for a few outings to give us an idea of rural life. We stayed at Avila for about two weeks and when our holiday was coming to a close, the priest in charge, Fr Collier, told us we could stay another day if wished, at Mount Melleray.

On arrival at Mount Melleray Mission next day, we found it was all locked up and nobody there. At that time our big treat was to be given a packet of sweets and a packet of biscuits, and we were glad to have these in Melleray as there was nothing else to eat, the convent being closed. We were lucky as we found a box room which had a small bed. It would do fine, we thought, and it did. We went to bed at the usual time; Sister Francesca slept at the top of the bed and I slept at the foot. All went fine until later in the night when Francesca called me and asked would I ever take my foot out of her mouth!

About six months after I arrived in Rhodesia, and having survived the initial mosquito attack, a newcomer came to invade my body. For a few days I noticed that there were red patches or lumps appearing here and there, particularly on my hip where the cincture or leather strap of our habit rested. They were quite sore; I didn't mind the soreness but wondered what they could be. Eventually I presented myself to the Sister in charge of sickbay, who thought they were boils and commenced immediately to give me injections. A few more days passed without any improvement and it was obvious the injections weren't the answer.

Finally, one morning after my bath, I discovered a large, fat worm working its way out through my skin. It had a black head on it. I was disgusted to know that he had been harbouring inside me, probably for a long time. At this stage there were several bumps so I thought there must be many more worms there. With a sterile needle I tried to remove some more which were not as large and they vanished eventually. I was told that the presence of the worms was due to the fact that I had worn clothes which had not been ironed after rain had fallen on them. Apparently the larvae of the tumbu or putse fly that lay their eggs on damp clothes that have not been fully ironed cause this disease. What a simple preventative, I thought, just make sure my clothes are properly ironed!

Every day brought something new to us in this country; on my first outing to the shops, accompanied by Sister Stanislaus, I certainly experienced something new. As Sister began to unload her basket of groceries and other essentials for the community, we heard someone call out, "One boy". An African man came running up to the counter, he put the goods into bags and waited until Sister paid her bill. He then followed us to our car and insisted on putting the bags in the car. I asked the Sister what was his name, but she didn't know. She said they were simply called 'boy'. A little later on I saw the different queues in banks and post offices. We had not been prepared for this situation before coming to Rhodesia and felt shocked at such racial segregation. The Sisters, however, treated the people with the greatest respect at all times and this respect was reciprocated.

When the schools closed we were given a holiday and this was wonderful because the mission schools closed at the same time. The older Sisters would have more time with us and we would go to different villages to see where the local people lived. Their mud huts were always spotless, despite the fact that the women had to draw buckets of water on their heads many times a day. They were kind and always insisted on serving us with cocoa or tea if they had it. What amazed me most was the lovely custom they had whereby food was never served without washing the hands; a basin of warm water and a clean towel were passed from one person to another and each washed their hands before eating. The fire was in the middle of the mud floor and the pots and pans all hung neatly along the walls.

The women did the cooking and all the digging for the crops and most families grew their own maize and would get it ground at the nearest mill. This would then be cooked to make *sadza* which formed the staple diet, and the woman had to be good and efficient at cooking the *sadza*, otherwise the husband might not consider her a good wife. With the *sadza*, meat (mostly chicken) and some type of green vegetables would be served. The family would sit around the fire, each one with a dish on the ground before them, they would then take a piece of *sadza* with their fingers, dip it into the sauce from the meat and vegetables and pop it into their mouths.

Gradually, during visits to Avila and Mount Melleray Missions, I was getting to know more people and becoming more friendly with them. On one occasion Sister Stanislaus and

I went for a cycle during our holiday, I have no idea where we got the bicycles which were men's bicycles but it didn't matter, it was just wonderful cycling around the countryside. As time went by in this new and wonderful country, I began to love it and to love the people and their simple way of life. I longed for the day when I would be working permanently at one of the mission stations and caring for the sick.

On our return trip from the mission stations we decided to visit a friend of mine called Aquilina, whom I knew from Mount Melleray Mission. She invited us in for tea, and before we left she told me she had a gift for me; she took us to the hen run and told me to pick one hen or *huku* in Shona (local language) and asked would I like it dead or alive. I decided I would like it alive and I was deeply grateful to her, as it was a great honour to be given such a gift. We got on our bikes and Aquilina fixed my *huku* nicely under my arm and on we went as happy as could be. We got somebody to kill the *huku* and we thoroughly enjoyed our lunch the following day.

Even though I was not yet doing my study, I was enjoying life, especially in the rural area. The more visits we made to the mission stations, the better we got to know the priests and they got to know us. On a few occasions we were invited over to their house for a cup of tea. They would offer us a glass of sherry but, as with the story of 'honey bunch', there was a danger that there could be a telltale in our midst. In spite of that, we enjoyed our sherry and hoped for the best. Mount Melleray was my favourite mission since it was there the pioneer Sisters lived and endured the hardships of those early years. The duration of our holidays was two weeks and we always got our packet of sweets and biscuits. We didn't mind, as the joy of getting out into the rural area was of far more importance than money or anything else.

The next holiday that Sister Francesca and I enjoyed was to Avila Mission station; we had already been there before, but just for a very short period. Avila was extremely low at just about 1,800ft. above sea level and water was a big problem there. A well had been dug in advance of the buildings being built but it failed and the community depended entirely on water from the river which was quite a distance from the mission. Monday mornings was the chosen time to go to the river for water to wash the clothes and, as the local people would say 'to wash the body', and to provide sufficient water for cooking and washing up. Away we would go with our large bath full of clothes, a container for water for domestic use, and a couple of long bars of blue soap, all in the back of the jeep. When the laundry was completely washed and rinsed it was put on the banks to dry before we returned to the mission. Then it was our turn to wash the body. Having chosen a sheltered and private spot, we each enjoyed our bath which was refreshing and invigorating.

Back at the mission convent, the Sisters had a filter in the kitchen to make sure the water was purified, but some time later two of the Sisters fell ill. Investigations were made, only to discover they both had bilharzia, a disease which had been contracted from the water snail in the river. Despite its appearance, the river was not sufficiently fast-flowing and bilharzia (also known as schistosomiasis) is caused by minute worms that infect certain species of fresh water snails found in the slow-flowing rivers, lakes and dams. Once inside the snail, they multiply for several weeks before being released into the water. The worms enter the body through the skin and attach themselves to the intestine or bladder. It takes months before the disease is established. Symptoms gradually emerge, including tiredness, pain and blood in the urine. In the early days, the treatment given was called ambilhar, but the side-effects of this treatment were drastic.

The affected Sisters were advised to stay indoors, away from sunlight – they were so terribly ill and scarcely able to eat or drink. Once the treatment was over they gradually recovered and soon gained their full strength. I had been with them when they were swimming, so I prayed I might have escaped this worm. But this was not to be, for sure enough, over a year later I began to experience the same symptoms as the other Sisters and on examination, an infection of bilharzia was confirmed. Luckily for me, at that stage a new treatment was available consisting of one injection of hycanthone, which killed the infection and had no side-effects. It still took some months, however, before I was returned to full health and energy.

About ten years after my arrival in Rhodesia, I discovered that my mother was finding it very difficult to write to me. Eventually, my sister Eileen told me the sad news that my mother was in early stages of Parkinson's disease. Doing a bit of research I discovered that it was a progressive disease, and could eventually lead to physical and mental illness.

Fortunately, in my mother's case, her mind was never affected. She had always had an active mind; she loved reading and listening to the radio and she encouraged us to do the same from when we were very young. I was anxious to visit home when I heard about my mother but the twenty-year ban on travelling home was still in place. However, I found out that there was such a thing as 'compassionate leave'. I approached my Superiors and asked for permission to go to Ireland to see my mother. The matter was discussed for some time and eventually permission was granted.

I flew from Salisbury to Shannon, where I was met by my sister Eileen and her husband, Jimmy. They were so kind, and did what they could to prepare me for the big change I was going to see in my mother. Telling a person, however, does not prepare one, and while I believed I would be ready for whatever was ahead, I got a huge shock when I saw my mother. The years and the illness had taken their toll on Mam; while her mind was perfect, her little body had become frail and she was so much smaller than she used to be. She was absolutely thrilled to see me again and I think it gave her a great boost.

My father, on the other hand, had not changed very much, except that he had gone grey. Mam's illness was a huge worry for him, but the family were a great help – Eileen and Jimmy, Bridie and her husband, Paddy, and Pa and his wife, Maureen, all gave a helping hand. My time at home was drawing to a close and the goodbyes were again hanging over me. Mam insisted on going to the airport with me; it was so sad and so difficult to have to say goodbye, and all the while I wondered if this would be the last time I would ever see her. I wept for the greater part of the journey back to Rhodesia and it took me some time to get over it. I relied all that time on prayer and Our Lady to help me through.

During this time, huge changes were taking place in the Church worldwide, with the advent of Vatican II under the guidance of Pope John XXIII. Many of the mission Superiors were near retirement age. They had worked extremely hard, both in India and Africa and while they were strict, that was not peculiar to the Presentation Order only. Mother Bernard returned to England to enjoy her retirement, while Mother Peter was appointed the new regional Superior for our region. Prior to her appointment, I had been sent to Mount Melleray to do my A Level studies privately and through correspondence. I enjoyed that time, and I also got the opportunity to help out in the hospital and outlying clinics at Mount Melleray, all of which was very good experience for someone who wanted to train as a nurse. My experience of applying myself to studying while in Penzance was a tremendous help.

I was helping out in the mission in Avila when I got news from my sister that my mother was not well. That letter was, I felt, preparing me for the worst. We didn't have a phone at the mission, so I knew the next message would have to be sent up with someone on the bus from Inyanga and that was, in fact, how I got the news that my mother was dead. Mam was dead at least a week before I knew. She passed away peacefully in hospital on October 9th, 1969, aged 73 and surrounded by my father and the rest of the family. It was hard being so very far from home, with nobody to talk to or to tell me how Mam had died, no chance to hold someone, or to tell them how much I had always loved and appreciated her, or to say goodbye. I had known she was in hospital, so her death was not entirely unexpected, but that did not take from the loneliness and the terrible feelings of loss I experienced.

The most vivid memories that kept coming to mind were of the mornings when we would leave the house to walk to school, and looking back to see Mam standing in the doorway, waving until we were out of sight. A lovely dinner awaited us each evening on our arrival home. It may not have been posh – it could be bacon rashers fried with onion, with milk or cream added – but it was simply delicious, with potatoes in a large dish in the centre of the table. There were lots of memories, but life goes on and each one copes as well as they possibly can. My father was still with us and now, thanks to Pope John XXIII and the relaxing of the twenty-year rule, I could count on another visit home sometime.

WORKING AS
A MISSION NURSE

Salisbury, Bulawayo and
Mount Melleray Mission, Nyanga

1971-1978

Having completed my A Levels, I was ready to start nursing training in 1971. The course was three years long and I studied at the Salisbury Central Hospital. I was given a lovely room in the nurses' home in the city and on my weekends off, Roger, the driver from St Michael's Convent, would collect me. Six others started training with me and over the three years we became the best of friends and were always ready to help each other. Even though I was the only nun in the group, I never felt isolated or left out of anything. One very tall girl called me 'Shorty', a name that stuck to me for the full three years of our training.

The training was difficult, tiring and stressful at times. Our tutor in the preliminary school was from Guy's Hospital in London. She was lovely; her help and advice guided us along the way and she was always ready to answer our queries. I decided there was only one way for me to deal with the training and that was to get stuck into it. I worked hard and I felt I had as good a chance of succeeding as anybody else. The fact that I was a nun was not a problem even though patients would occasionally take a second look at me and wonder what I was doing there among so many young students. Time sorted all that out as I gained more self-confidence.

Without a car, I had to cycle most mornings in order to get Mass at the local cathedral. The long cycle and steep hill made me tired before the work started at all, but it was imperative that nuns get daily Mass. Sometimes I found the stress and strain of work, study, exams and weekly assessments, with night duty every few months, a bit much. The nights off were a huge bonus and energised us for the coming weeks. The three years went by quickly, but not without their ups and downs, joys and sorrows. Nursing is a job that brings one very close to people, not just in a physical way but also in a psychological and spiritual way. One is in a position to console, to quietly listen and, where necessary, to be of assistance during a patient's last moments.

On a few occasions I felt that a number of my patients were waiting for my arrival back on duty, just to be with them and perhaps to hold their hand, before they passed away. What a wonderful privilege that was for me. I was lucky as I felt that God was very near during those last moments, and it was that feeling that gave me the courage to continue. I found that there is a serene sense of dignity experienced by people who are comforted as they journey through the last moments of life. There is something special, a consoling sensation from the gentle sense of touch that appears to be so comforting during those moments. I was truly privileged to be present with people at such times.

We worked hard and felt that we deserved to pass our exams and, thankfully, we all did. It was just lovely that the entire group passed. Champagne flowed as the tutors celebrated with us. The goodbyes followed shortly afterwards as we each set off to pursue the next part of our life journey. I have always experienced a degree of sadness when parting with friends when the time comes to go our separate ways. I feel that genuine friendships, established along the laneway of life, occupy a special place in the secret chambers of the heart, and that always makes parting a difficult experience.

Having successfully completed that section of my exams, the next and final part was midwifery, which was necessary to complete before going out to the rural areas. After a few days' rest, I flew from Salisbury to the city of Bulawayo in Matabeleland where my one-year midwifery course was to take place. Once again I took up residence in the nurses' home and this time there were eight students in the group, consisting of five Africans and three Europeans. Mpilo Hospital, where we were training, catered for a very large population so we were extremely busy.

The manual work, such as the making of beds and turning patients, was tiring. The study was difficult but our tutor was artistic and she illustrated a good deal of the work on the board, which helped to simplify much of it. I found it most interesting to follow the life of a human being from the moment of conception to birth; the hormonal activity is just amazing in the development of the foetus. The oral and practical exams were made more difficult because of the language, but an interpreter was provided where necessary. The language in Matabeleland is totally different from the Shona language of Rhodesia with which I was fairly familiar.

On my days off, I would visit the various convents in the area and spend some time with the Sisters there. With them I visited the famous medieval stone ruins, Great Zimbabwe, from which the country was later to take its name at Independence. The Sisters took me to see many sites, including a game reserve, and it was enjoyable to get a break from the hospital and to meet many more people. Bulawayo is a city rich in history and surrounded by natural beauty. I found the people to be friendly, kind and very understanding where language issues were concerned. I managed to learn a few of the greetings in the native language which was most important. I discovered that African people like to be greeted properly, and not in a rushed manner as I had been inclined to do. Experience is a great teacher.

Great care was given to the patients, despite the fact that on occasion the hospital would be full to capacity. The matron and many of the tutors were British, as were some of the surgeons. Many junior doctors were from the locality, with some from other countries, including a few Irish. Due to the vast intake of patients, larger hospitals such as those in Salisbury and Bulawayo provided valuable experience for the junior doctors, experience they would not get elsewhere. Midwifery was an interesting course and consisted of a lot of very hard work and intense study. Assessments and oral exams meant that there was little time for pleasure. Nurses were required to assist at one hundred births before being allowed to take the final exams. House doctors were always nearby to assist when difficulties arose, such as foetal heart distress, or other problems where the nurse felt that the situation required the doctors' input.

Sadly, patients often came in for delivery without having had food for a number of days. Consequently they had very little energy or strength to push at the required time. This made the process extremely difficult for the baby, mother and nurse on duty. I have never felt what it must be like to be starving, but many of those expectant women did, and it was something that upset me greatly. The matron very kindly ensured that a flask of tea was available at all times. This was a help but it would not fill an empty stomach. Occasionally it gave me great joy to be able to help by giving my sandwiches to a patient. Another trick of mine was to offer the cook a cardigan or some nice item of clothing in exchange for some *sadza,* and it always worked out well, thankfully.

My friend next door in the nurses' home was also a nun. She started the course six months later than the rest of the group and was a delightful companion to have. Sister Angela was prayerful, caring and generous; I knew I could rely on her prayers and, in addition, she would help me with revision. Sister came from Germany and we had much to share about our diverse backgrounds. After some months, exam time was drawing near and, as with all students, the nerves were setting in. What I feared most was the practical exam – would I be able to give the examiner the correct outline of the foetus, the correct lie and position of the foetus, to feel the head and to listen to the foetal heart and, finally, to determine the expected date of delivery? Thankfully, everything went well. A date was set for the announcement of the results, and students were summoned individually to the matron's office. This was one occasion I shall never forget. I was sent for and, as I entered the matron's office, I saw her outstretched hand and smiling face as she cheerfully said, "Congratulations".

I was delighted at passing the final exam and it was a wonderful occasion for me, full of joy, excitement and gratitude to that lovely lady, the matron, who shared the joy with me. Later that evening the staff, surgeons and matron joined with us in our celebrations. The sad moment would soon follow when we each said our farewells and wished each other luck in the life that lay ahead. No matter how often I do it, I never get used to the void caused by the pangs of parting. But nothing stands still, and from that day forward all responsibility would rest on our own shoulders, with no tutor to turn to, and no surgeon to rely on. Yet, I knew that the good training that we received at Mpilo Hospital would give us confidence and courage when situations were difficult.

As I was about to board a plane back to Salisbury, I gave a last look at the training hospital and in my heart I felt anxious, apprehensive and, in a sense, a little lonely. I knew I would shortly be taking over a mission hospital which had been run

Margaret, pictured on a visit home to Ireland in 1978, with niece Mary and brother Pa.

Outlying clinic at Tsoko from St Therese's Mission in Chiduku, 1980. Here there were 117 patients presenting for ante-natal care and injections as well as with general illnesses. Each outlying clinic was visited weekly and the venue provided an occasion of social encounter for the local people.

Bill and his mother, Eileen Noonan, early 1980s.

Bill and Margaret after their wedding ceremony in Rome in 1986.

Margaret at home after her marriage in Rome in 1986.

*Judy with Margaret's grandniece, Linda,
in Tarbert, Co Kerry, in the late 1980s.*

by the Presentation Sisters for many years. Amidst poverty, drought, heat and insects, great work had been done by the missionaries. Many lives had been saved by these dedicated people who gave of their best. I felt as I always did – that the Lord would be with me as I set out for Mount Melleray Mission where the Sisters had started their work in 1949.

Great joy awaited me as I approached Mount Melleray Mission at the foot of the Mosie mountain. Mother Peter would be my companion and helper; my mind was set at ease immediately when Mother told me she would continue in the hospital with me until I settled in. Mother was a very experienced nurse who had trained in India. Her reputation was known far and wide for the tremendous work she had done. I knew only too well that I could never follow in her footsteps, but her advice and assistance were invaluable. Although I had been to Melleray many times before, it was now to be my home and I grew to truly love the place. Around the mission area, the scent of flowering trees and shrubs wafted continuously, the gentle breeze blowing this way and that helped keep us cool, and all of this was crowned with heavenly sunshine from a cloudless, blue sky. The natural beauty of the place was truly a sight to behold, and one for which I thanked God. It was mine to enjoy and, having a love for nature all my life, this was truly divine.

After a day or two I began to work in the hospital with the assistance of Mother Peter. We had a beautiful shortcut to the hospital, with each side of it laden with shrubs and trees which filled one with a sense of serenity, peace and joy. On guard duty at the hospital were two beautiful dogs, known as

Mother Peter's pets. One was an Alsatian and the other was a Rhodesian Ridgeback and they were wonderful company. A little orphan girl was being taken care of at the hospital; each morning she was put in her cot and taken out on to the open verandah where she would benefit from the fresh air and lovely sunshine. She was never alone as the Alsatian lay on the ground beside her – how safe and snug she looked.

As the days went by, I began to gain some confidence and soon found myself falling into the routine established by Mother Peter. Three times a week we attended the outlying clinics. These were held in the same places each time; a date would have been given and patients would be guided for time by the sun. For shelter we chose a very large tree and the back of the ambulance formed a table, while ante-natal patients were checked out in a nearby hut. Many patients' lives were saved through these clinics.

I recall a woman who got badly burned at home. She was a long distance from the clinic, so the family placed her in a wheelbarrow and brought her along. We made her as comfortable as possible in the ambulance, and Mother Peter told me to take her to the hospital in Mount Melleray immediately. Thankfully, after a lot of care and nourishment, she began to heal again. I remembered the story Mother had told long before that about the gentleman who had walked miles to get to the hospital with twins in a suitcase. The following day the mother travelled that awful distance hoping against hope that her babies were still alive. Mother Peter made sure that they were. Both parents and babies went home very grateful and extremely happy.

As time passed, I gradually became accustomed to the routine. I just loved the place; Mother Peter was a joy to work with and the patients were grateful for the care and attention they were receiving. Relatives of our patients would accompany them when they were admitted to the wards. The hospital had an outdoor house arranged so that the relatives could see to the cooking. Small fires were lit for cooking pots, vegetables were prepared and the patients were well taken care of. But there were worrying times also, especially with maternity cases. A doctor visited the hospital once a month, which was a tremendous help, but when a serious situation arose it was necessary to go to the hospital in Nyanga, which was about twenty miles away. It was a long journey if the patient was very ill, and occasionally the priest would do the driving for us, as one would have to stay in the back of the vehicle with the patient. Despite any difficulties, life went on very happily for Mother Peter and me. We treated ourselves to a game of scrabble after a long day's work, as we both loved it and found it a great method of relaxation before going to bed.

After some time at Mount Melleray, Mother Peter advised me to have a break and go to Avila Mission, which I was delighted to do, as I loved that place also. I spent a few days there and when returning to Mount Melleray, the priest at Avila, Fr Collier, kindly offered to drive me back, as he was going to the local town, Nyanga, to do some shopping and then travelling on to Salisbury. Following my return, I was coming from the church to the convent and en route I met a French-Canadian Brother who lived near us. He informed me that he had a letter for Fr Collier which contained news of a death. He said it was from someone called Irene. I told him that I knew of most of Fr Collier's immediate family, but no one with that name. I assured Brother that I would give Fr Collier the letter when he stopped at Mount Melleray on his way back to Avila. I later decided that I should give Fr Collier the information over the phone, in case he needed to make a call home. There wasn't a phone at his mission and it would be easier for him to make contact from Salisbury where was staying for a couple of days.

Eventually I managed to reach him. I opened the letter and proceeded to pass on the details. It read as follows: 'Please tell Madge that Dad has died, signed Eileen'. I was dumbfounded; I kept reading the letter and eventually realised that it must be for me. The names 'Eileen' and 'Madge' were our family names, and not those of Fr Collier. Being so very far from home with poor communication made it all the more difficult. I took the letter to Mother Peter and she felt my loss very deeply also. It was very difficult to phone Ireland from where we were, so Fr Collier very kindly offered to take me to Salisbury where I could phone home. We did this and eventually we managed to get my sister Eileen.

She told me that Dad had been watching the Grand National, sitting on an armchair in the kitchen. He must have got a sudden pain and gone to his bedroom, as he was found lying back on the bed. It was a huge relief for me to know that he died at home, as one tends to imagine all sorts of things when one is far from home. The shock and the loneliness were awful, as my mother had died just a year and half earlier. Apart from the loss of both of my wonderful parents, whom I loved so much, I now no longer had a home to go to. My sisters and brother were wonderful, but my original home was gone forever, and I really felt that the separation between my life in Rhodesia and my life in Ireland now took on a whole new meaning, and that voices I longed to hear were stilled forever.

This realisation took its toll on me and while everyone around me behaved in an extremely understanding manner, showing the utmost kindness, at such a time one naturally wants to talk to or be with family. The family bond is very special during times of sadness, but my family were thousands of miles away and I missed them hugely at this time. I was extremely lonely and missed both of my parents desperately. I was aware that each person has the same experiences at some time in their lives and so, in time, I pulled myself together. Life and work continued, and I found that helping others is the best form of therapy when times are tough and things are not what we would wish them to be.

As the number of patients increased, Mother Peter decided it was necessary to employ more nurses. At that stage, local people were getting more and more access to education, some were doing nursing, while others opted for teaching, and still others studied medicine. Salisbury had a large university and the local people were now in a position to avail of its teaching facilities. The university was situated directly across from our convent at St Michael's. There were a number of girls in our mission who had completed their school years and had obtained a reasonable standard of English language proficiency. They worked as cleaners in the hospital at Mount Melleray and it bothered me to see those lovely young girls who did the cleaning and other minor chores not utilising their brains in a way that would benefit not just themselves, but also their country.

One day I was speaking to Mother Peter and we discussed this and wondered what we could do. I came up with the idea of teaching the girls a course in First Aid. Mother agreed she would undertake the practical side of it and I would see to the oral and written papers, and we were able to use the nurses' home (the Sister whom I had replaced in Mount Melleray had managed to get a nurses' home built with aid from an Irish organisation). We instigated a course and the girls were overjoyed to get an opportunity to be part of our initiative, and took to it like ducks to water. We proceeded with the course and insisted on punctuality and stressed the fact that we expected the girls to give due attention to homework. We had no problems whatsoever as the students were extremely anxious to study and to get something out of life. They were put through their exams by two outside examiners and the Red Cross awarded them their certificates. They were delighted with this achievement and so were Mother Peter and I.

The girls did not want to stop there, so on went our thinking caps once more. I had a few certificates for typing and thought perhaps that I could use that bit of knowledge to some advantage. Without typewriters it would be difficult, but I knew that the European schools were now beginning to teach Commercial subjects to African students. I approached the Sisters and, after a good deal of begging, I returned with one portable typewriter and some typing paper. Better than nothing, I thought! Having talked with the students, I discovered that they loved the idea, even though they had never seen a typewriter. That made no difference to them or to me. Determination was all that was required and they had that in abundance.

I explained to them that an examination would be carried out where they would have to type twenty-five accurate words in a minute. In time, this was all done. Prior arrangements were made with a tutor at a Pitman training centre in England who agreed to correct the papers and, if the students were successful, they would be issued with the appropriate certificates. The students were wonderful and, in turn, each one received a certificate and those certificates gave them a wonderful start in life. Eventually I was allowed to set the exam dates myself, and I did this while I was working at Mount Melleray Mission.

Shared occasions of joy in the mission outposts gave us missionaries a great sense of togetherness in what was sometimes a lonely existence. Many years prior to my arrival at Mount Melleray Mission, a lovely custom had developed in many of the rural missions. A couple of times a year, the priest in charge would throw a party and invite members from as many neighbouring mission stations as possible. The evening would start with the Office of the day or some type of evening prayer. A lovely meal followed, with a drink or a glass of wine (what a joy!). An atmosphere of joy, excitement and relaxation prevailed for the evening. The best was to follow when the table and chairs were put aside, the music started and records from home were played on a record player, and the mood was set for dancing.

Proceedings usually started with the old time waltz and I distinctly recall the change that came over my entire body when I was dancing. To feel the touch of another human gave me a warm, loving feeling that I wished would last forever. We danced through the night and stopped only when someone sang a song or told a story. Joy shone on all the faces and I wondered if others felt as I did. This practice continued for many years and each party was wonderful, giving a sense of warmth and belonging. I longed for that human touch every time; to simply feel the warmth of another body close to mine had a profound effect on me. In my heart, I felt deeply for all those other nuns who weren't invited to the parties and who, perhaps, never experienced the affection or love of another human being. Love, I believe, comes from God and, if used correctly, can be a wonderful way of honouring God's presence in our lives.

GROWING UNREST

Rhodesia

Mid – late 1970s

Although our lives were relatively peaceful, there had been unrest in the country for many years. Racial discrimination prevailed throughout the region and while the white Rhodesians and immigrants held the country's wealth and positions of power, African people were suppressed and denied their rights. They were not allowed into hotels, swimming pools and other such public places. African girls who joined religious orders and were out for a day to celebrate some occasion or other would not be allowed to join the white Sisters in a restaurant or hotel. To avoid this situation, the Sisters would take a picnic and have their celebration in a park or some such place where there was no racial discrimination.

Back in 1965, the prime minister, Ian Smith, and his government had decided to issue a Unilateral Declaration of Independence (UDI). This came about mainly because there had been disagreement between the British government, led by Harold Wilson, and the Smith government. The Church, which had always championed the cause of the oppressed where possible, felt it could no longer sit back and watch the rampant injustices. The bishops opposed UDI and they spoke out and wrote about it. Bishop Donal Lamont, the first bishop of Umtali, was one of its greatest critics.

Bishop Lamont was born in County Antrim in the early twentieth century and in 1946 had been appointed the Superior of the Carmelite Mission in Rhodesia. He was an outspoken man and a resolute opponent of social and political discrimination in the country. Shortly after becoming bishop he decided it was time to consider the need to formally denounce the system of racial discrimination, and he issued his personal manifesto, 'Purchased People', in his pastoral letter. Many more letters were written in the following years and the final one before Independence was written in 1978, entitled 'A Plea for Reconciliation'.

In the meantime, we were wondering what lay ahead of us. We continued working, even in the most remote outlying clinics. By 1975 there was growing unrest, and the rumblings of national unrest were apparent. At this stage we had no idea of what was going to happen or what the two rebel leaders, Robert Mugabe (ZANU) and Joshua Nkomo (ZAPU), were planning. We guessed that sooner or later war would start and it did. They started their raids and decided to strike deep in the heart of the countryside. The ferocity of the strikes affected many white people, many of whom had been born in Africa and knew no other home but Rhodesia. Many left their homes and farms, especially people living in the Eastern Highlands.

We, as missionaries, wondered if we would escape, as we were not involved in politics, although we disagreed with the system of racial discrimination. As in all wars, however, the Church was bound to suffer and in Rhodesia it surely did. Very soon hatred flourished, bringing with it great fear, distrust and tension. The government laid down laws stating that the presence of freedom fighters had to be reported to the security forces. Very severe penalties would be enforced individually and collectively if this was not done. Bishop Lamont told all of us to give medicine to the wounded if requested. This was totally against the law, but he was prepared to take full responsibility for our actions. That was fine with us, but we knew that Bishop Lamont would be many miles away if and when such an occasion arose.

Young boys from the schools were going over Mosie mountain and into Mozambique to be trained in the art of warfare. The teaching Sisters would have known many of the students and feared greatly for their safety. Other students would have been known from the hospitals. I felt deeply for the parents who would wake up to find that their lovely sons were gone from their home. They knew it was probably to go over the border to be trained to use weapons and, sadly, many never returned. The police force was mixed with several different nationalities within its ranks, some of whom were Irish, but, on occasion, this was of no benefit to us – war is war. Many villages were being attacked and innocent men, women and children were needlessly killed. People in some areas were herded into 'keeps' and were allowed out only to see their cattle.

No sympathy or understanding was shown to the missionaries by the security forces. The diocesan priests were treated very badly simply because they were black, and many of our Irish priests were intimidated, imprisoned and later deported back to Ireland. Many mission stations were without telephones and yet the missionaries were expected to report the presence of freedom fighters. Despite our fears, Mother Peter and I continued to work both in the hospital and in the outlying clinics. Occasionally, I could see the fear in Mother's face. She was no longer young, but I knew it would break her heart to leave her beloved Mount Melleray. Day after day we struggled along, but the situation was getting worse all the time and more and more lives were being lost. In addition to our work, we had to travel long distances to attend court when our Carmelite priests were being tried for offences for which they were not responsible.

We also felt that we should support the priests who were being deported, and we were very sad to see them being treated so unfairly. In 1977, two Carmelite priests were shot at and one got shrapnel in his back and had to go to Ireland for treatment. He returned later to resume his work and, while his condition was not great, he wanted to be with his people in their time of need. In the case of the other priest, a bullet penetrated his shoulder and came out the collar bone. He also required treatment in Ireland and, again, in time returned to his post. Pastoral work became almost impossible, but the people understood that we were with them in their struggle and they feared for our safety.

White farmers were being killed frequently, many of whom we would have known through the schools. In 1979, two more Carmelite priests were taken out at gunpoint; it was midnight and for a very long period of time they were kept on the verandah and were constantly threatened that they would be shot. Only intense persuasion and somebody's prayers prevented the triggers from being pulled. This type of situation existed throughout the entire country and, naturally, Mother Peter and I, like all the other missionaries, were feeling the tension and the fear. Going to the hospital by night was beginning to worry us, but we continued.

Despite our fears, we would often sit on the verandah in the evening, looking out at the brilliant colours of the shrubs, trees and bushes. But our greatest treasure of all remained the lovely little stream which flowed close by the hedge. The stream originated in the Mosie mountain and flowed very close to the mission. It was a lifesaver from the day the first missionaries arrived at Mount Melleray as there was no other source of water. Each day we used the water from that stream even though we had, at this stage, a water supply for the hospital and the convent. Lines from Tennyson's poem, 'The Brook', often came to mind: 'I chatter, chatter as I flow/to join the brimming river/for men may come and men may go/but I go on forever'. Despite what was happening all around us, Mother and I often asked each other how we could leave a place as wonderful as this?

War was taking hold in the country and many lives were being taken every day and night; we feared not only for our own lives, but for those of all the missionaries. Landmines were planted and we were warned to watch out for dung heaps or mounds of soil. Since we didn't have a resident doctor it was necessary for us to take our expectant mothers and seriously ill patients to the hospital in Nyanga, which was about 25 miles away. The road was rough and bumpy and flooded during the rainy season. On one occasion Mother Peter and I were returning from Nyanga after a pelvic assessment of an expectant woman. As we approached a bridge that was about 12 miles from the mission, we were stopped by the security forces. At first I felt nervous, as I was driving and wondered what I could have done that was out of order. They told me to leave the ambulance, which was a Datsun truck that had been converted into an ambulance, with a drip and other necessities installed. I got my driving licence and we got out of the truck.

However, it was not the vehicle itself that bothered them, but the fact that I had driven over a landmine which had not detonated. The forces were amazed that the landmine did not detonate given the weight of the truck. They took me along to show me the tracks of my vehicle on the landmine. I was shocked and Mother Peter was upset, as we both were aware that we would have to travel that same road again, and frequently. On another occasion as we travelled that road with patients, we were again ordered to stop by the security forces. This time they were removing another landmine and, had we been a few minutes earlier, we would have driven over it. We felt that our guardian angels were looking after us, not only then, but on many more occasions that were to follow.

Day by day the situation was getting more dangerous, more frightening and more worrying. The area where Mount

Melleray was, at the foot of the Mosie mountain and bordering Mozambique, provided a thoroughfare for both the security forces and the freedom fighters, and was the reason why the Nyanga roads were so dangerous. Bishop Lamont kept on talking publicly about the situation in the country, both in local papers and in foreign media. He also kept telling us not to refuse to give medicine or treatment to the freedom fighters. Giving treatment could cause the security forces and the government to impose the death penalty, jail or deportation. We now feared both sides equally as, if we refused to treat the freedom fighters, they could very easily shoot.

Eventually the government ordered Bishop Lamont to be brought before the court in Umtali. At this stage Mother Peter and I, as well as other missionaries, were constantly attending court in an effort to support our innocent priests, and now the bishop. Bishop Lamont was sentenced to ten years in jail. However, he wasn't actually put in jail as the government feared bad publicity, nationally and internationally, and so, instead, they deported him back to Ireland. That was a shock for him and for all of us. We saw the bishop off at the airport and I'm sure that he very much disliked having to leave Rhodesia at a very critical stage in its history.

The war was destroying people and places and we didn't know what was going to happen next. There were two Sisters and one priest stationed at Avila Mission about fifty miles north of us. They didn't have a phone and mail was available only when the bus managed to travel those awful roads. Nobody called to see if they were all right and if they had all the necessities they needed. I thought it would be easier for me to go and see them rather that to be worrying about them at night. Dear Mother Peter and Fr Joseph (the priest in charge of Mount Melleray Mission) were anxious to come with me. We were well aware that the long journey had many hazards, including being stopped, turned back and, worse still, the dangers of landmines or being attacked.

On the morning we had decided to undertake the journey, Father Joseph agreed to go to our nearest village to collect mail for the Sisters and to buy bread and some meat for them. While we waited for his return, I went to church to recite the Office of the day. The psalm for that day was one I had repeated on Thursdays for many years before, but the wonderful significance of the words had never struck me as forcefully as they did on that occasion:

Alone with none but Thee, my God,
I journey on my way.
What need I fear, when Thou art near,
O King of night and day?
More safe am I within Thy hand
Than if a host did round me stand.
My destined time is fixed by Thee,
And Death doth know his hour.
Did warriors strong around me throng,
They could not stay his power.
No walls of stone can man defend
When Thou Thy messenger dost send.

My life I yield to Thy decree,
And bow to Thy control
In peaceful calm, for from Thine arm
No power can wrest my soul.
Could earthly omens e'er appal
A man that heeds the heavenly call?
The child of God can fear no ill,
His chosen dread no foe;
We leave our fate with Thee, and wait
Thy bidding when to go.
'Tis not from chance our comfort springs.
Thou art our trust, O King of kings.

I found that psalm gave me courage and absolute trust in God's loving protection, not only for me, but for all the missionaries travelling the unsafe roads.

We set off when all was packed and ready, not knowing that the security forces were not only on the roads with their large army trucks, but were actually situated on the hillside across from our mission at Mount Melleray. We knew that they were aware of all our movements. They stopped us on a few occasions after leaving the mission and informed us that many of their trucks had been blown up by landmines in the area. We already knew this, as we saw the trucks being towed away. Each time they stopped us that day, we informed them that we were going, and nothing would stop us. We were travelling in a Peugeot car, and we knew that the lighter the vehicle, the less the danger of detonation if we drove over a landmine.

After about two hours we finally arrived at our destination. The Sisters and the priest at Avila could scarcely believe what they were seeing. Their mail from home was so welcome, as well as the bit of food and, of course, there was great joy at seeing us and finding out how we were getting on. We had something to eat but did not delay very long as we felt it would be easier to detect landmines in the daylight. We returned home feeling happy that they were well, but we were very disturbed at some of the stories we had heard.

They told us that a group of freedom fighters had arrived to the mission at Avila one evening and demanded that the missionaries go with them up the side of the hill. When they all had assembled, the fighters asked the local people if they would like to have the missionaries shot. In shock, the people shouted not to touch the missionaries. Such stories were disturbing and a cause of worry, and all the more so because Avila Mission was so remote and without any means of communication. Sometime later the Superiors in Ireland insisted that the Sisters leave the mission and return to Ireland. They did so, but felt very lonely leaving their people in the hospital and in the schools, where they had served for many years and where they had been extremely happy.

Fighting throughout the country became more ferocious, and deaths were a daily occurrence. The happy evenings sitting out on the verandahs, and those magical evenings when we let our hair down at the mission station parties, were gone. There were many more shocks awaiting us. Fr Patrick, who looked after the two Sisters we visited in Avila, was arrested for not reporting the presence of freedom fighters who visited the mission. If he had wished to do so, he wouldn't have been able, as he had no means of contacting anyone since there was no phone or means of communication whatsoever. He was arrested, taken to court and imprisoned.

Being African, he was treated very badly. Despite the danger of landmines, we visited him daily and brought him tea and sandwiches. On some occasions we were allowed to speak to him, but only through barbed wire. When I asked if he could sleep by night, he replied that it was impossible because of the heat, and the prisoners were packed like sardines in a tin. Fr Patrick was later removed to another prison which was out of our reach. I felt that deeply, as he was a very gentle, kind person. He loved to read but, with the poor lighting, neither he nor any of the other prisoners could do so.

Mother Peter and I tried to continue our routine, being ever watchful for landmines on the roads. A type of propaganda was spreading about the country that the government and the security forces were winning the war, that their number of casualties was less than that of the freedom fighters. Prime Minister Ian Smith often repeated that there would never be African rule. He and his government were very well-protected but the missionaries had neither protection nor security and were targets from both sides. Our Superiors told us we could leave the war situation and return to Ireland at any time if we felt the pressure was too great. I knew in my heart that I could never do that – I was responsible for the hospital, and I was determined to stay there.

At one point Fr Joseph, Mother Peter and I had a horrific experience. A lovely, older couple lived close to our mission. The husband was from South Africa and the wife was Irish, from Tralee in County Kerry, and they had one son who was a charming young man. They were our neighbours, and our dear friends, and each Sunday they attended our church for Mass. This was followed by a cup of tea across the yard in the convent where we always enjoyed a good old chat, and never at any time did they give the impression that they were worried about the situation. As events unfolded, we discovered that they were very worried and had tried to take precautions.

We would go shopping to Nyanga town about once a week and we always called to see them and ask if they needed anything. On this occasion, the three of us, Fr Joseph, Mother Peter and I, stopped at our neighbours' house as usual. Father and I went in to see them and, fortunately, Mother Peter remained in the car. What we saw in the house was a terrible sight to behold. Both of them had been shot several times and there was blood all over the place. The wife's little body, and little she was, was scarcely recognisable. Inside the door were bags of maize which they mistakenly thought would protect them. Our initial reaction was severe shock and utter heartbreak for our dear friends. We were also very frightened, because we didn't know when this massacre had taken place or if the murderers were still about.

We informed Mother Peter and returned to the mission immediately to report our gruesome discovery to the police. We tried to cope with the shock and get on with our own lives. We knew we were in danger as there were no other Europeans close to us, and the ferocity of this slaying was a stark reminder of the horror and outrage that were tearing this lovely country apart. The couple's near neighbours told us they had heard shooting during the night and, as a result, all our nights from then on were fearful and worrying. From six o'clock onwards, we didn't have light or electricity, as the generator had to be turned off, and we depended on torches and candles for hospital and general work.

I distinctly recall the many nights we sat on the verandah listening for every sound. I felt I had to investigate every rattle or noise. Many times we saw flares going up indicating that there was trouble somewhere in the vicinity. Yet life had to go on; practically every day we would get word that an African neighbour had been either imprisoned or shot. They, too, were being accused of not reporting the presence of freedom fighters in their area. Like us, it was impossible for them to do that, and if they did and the freedom fighters heard about it, they suffered punishment, imprisonment or death.

When visiting the local prison in Nyanga where our priests were held, Mother Peter and myself often saw the dead bodies of those who had been shot. English missionaries who lived near Avila Mission and who were dear friends spent some time in prayer and reflection wondering if they should move to a safer situation. They moved to Umtali where they were all massacred. A monument was later erected in their memory which reads, 'My Father, I do not understand You, but I trust You'.

Another life of one who had devoted himself to the poor
was brutally taken. John Bradburn was an Englishman who
had devoted practically all his life to caring for people in many
different ways. He had spent many, many years living in a hut,
and taking care of the lepers in a colony situated in Mtoko
outside Salisbury. The Irish Franciscan priests knew him very
well and our Sisters often helped at the colony during the
holidays. News of his death was just not credible. Why would
anyone shoot a very saintly person such as he was? At one stage
in his life, John had asked the Franciscan priests if he could be
laid out in the Franciscan habit. With the terrible shock of his
sudden death by shooting, and the fuss surrounding it, nobody
thought of the habit.

One priest, who lived a good distance away, heard the news
by bush telegram and immediately made his way to where
John lay. He insisted on opening the coffin and laid John out
in the Franciscan habit as had been his wish. He was taken to
the church in Salisbury and extraordinary things seem to have
happened there. Blood was seen to drop from the coffin at the
Consecration of the Mass. Sadly, I was unable to attend the
Mass or funeral. Sometime later a Franciscan priest wrote an
account of John's life which was published.

Despite all the horror, we tried to remain cheerful for our
patients and for ourselves. Mother Peter and I continued to
enjoy our evening game of scrabble and would occasionally
phone the Sisters in Salisbury to let them know how we were.
They were aware of all the difficulties we were encountering
and one of them very kindly offered to relieve me for a couple

of days, so we exchanged places. The change was most welcome and helped me to forget the situation for a little while. Life was not all sunshine in Salisbury either, but they did not have to contend with landmines and other difficulties experienced in the outpost missions.

Shortly after, my Superior decided it was time I made a retreat. There was one being conducted by a German Jesuit in Mtoko, so she made arrangements for me to attend it. The retreat was inspiring, relaxing and most helpful in the situation in which we found ourselves. The priest, Fr Shepherd-Smith, interviewed each one of us daily and chose Scripture passages for us to study privately for the interview the following day. The retreat lasted seven days, seven most inspiring days and at the end of each day Fr Shepherd-Smith would close with the hymn 'Amazing Grace', which continues to have a special place in my heart.

> *Amazing grace! How sweet the sound*
> *That saved a wretch like me!*
> *I once was lost, but now am found;*
> *Was blind, but now I see.*
> *'Twas grace that taught my heart to fear,*
> *And grace my fears relieved;*
> *How precious did that grace appear*
> *The hour I first believed.*
> *Through many dangers, toils and snares,*
> *I have already come;*
> *'Tis grace hath brought me safe thus far,*

And grace will lead me home.
The Lord has promised good to me,
His word my hope secures;
He will my shield and portion be,
As long as life endures.
Yea, when this flesh and heart shall fail,
And mortal life shall cease,
I shall possess, within the veil,
A life of joy and peace.
The world shall soon dissolve like snow,
The sun refuse to shine;
But God, who called me here below,
Shall be forever mine.
When we've been there ten thousand years,
Bright shining as the sun,
We've no less days to sing God's praise
Than when we'd first begun.

I returned home to my mission after the retreat, and a few days later I learned that our newly appointed Superior General in Ireland had decided to visit us in Rhodesia. When she arrived, arrangements were made that I meet her and the local Superior on the main road before entering the dirt road, as the ambulance which I used was well-known in the area. After our initial greetings, they asked me to sit into their car just for a moment. There they told me that the priest who had conducted the retreat I had recently undertaken, Fr Shepherd-Smith, had been shot dead. He was visiting a neighbouring mission one evening for a chat, when he and the other priests and a number of elderly Sisters were taken out, put standing by a hedge and all shot dead. Needless to say, I was horrified, hurt and lonely, and I wondered who would be the next victim of this war. Each time I hear 'Amazing Grace' my thoughts immediately go to that priest and to all the others who were so brutally taken from us.

When our priest in charge of the mission at Mount Melleray found himself in deep trouble, his Superior and all of us encouraged him to leave and to return to Ireland. Even though we were very sad and missed him terribly, we were much happier in the knowledge that he was safe. Mother Peter was beginning to feel the strain also and her sleep was being affected. That was a huge worry for me. We talked a lot and prayed about it and eventually Mother thought it was better to go home. When the Superior from Ireland spoke with me, she said that she could not possibly ask someone from Ireland to come out and stay with me. I insisted that there was no necessity whatsoever, and I told her I was staying come what may. If they wanted to shoot me, I reasoned, well, it would be fast, and we all have to die at some stage. I would not have liked to have been dragged over the mountain to care for wounded freedom fighters. Fortunately it did not happen, in my case anyway, or to any of our Sisters.

At this time Mount Melleray Mission was the only mission station still open and I was the only Presentation Sister out in the rural area. Some Sisters from St Benedict's Mission station went home, just for a holiday, and were told not to return as their mission had to be closed. That was horrible for them as their jobs and all their possessions were gone so suddenly. After a short time on my own, a Sister from Nagle House Convent, Sister Ancilla, came to join me at Mount Melleray as she had a throat problem and could not continue teaching at the school at Nagle House. What a joy for me just to have someone to talk to. She even accompanied me by night to the hospital. Another priest, Fr Liam, was sent to our mission. Fr Liam insisted on sleeping in the older section of the convent while Sister Ancilla and I used two new rooms which had been added some time earlier.

Casualties were being reported daily and during such times the promise of a bag of sugar, or even a bar of soap, would be sufficient to entice someone to report the presence of freedom fighters, as regard for human life on both sides was practically non-existent. As the situation worsened, Fr Liam insisted on accompanying us at night on hospital calls, and he drove the truck. At that stage it was almost impossible to know who was who, but if there were freedom fighters about, Father was prepared to take responsibility for our actions. Eventually the big blow for us came when Ian Smith's government forbade any white people to remain on in rural areas. I thought my heart would break at the thought of leaving my hospital, our little orphan and all our patients, both in the central mission and in the outlying clinics.

Although our visits there were infrequent by this stage, the people knew we were still in the area. I thought I would have to put down our two beautiful dogs, the Alsatian and the lovely Rhodesian Ridgeback but, happily, our local doctor, Doctor Knight, offered to take them for us. Shortly after the government's edict, Sister Ancilla and I had to pack up our belongings and try to secure the convent as well as we could for our departure. The saddest part of all was having to lock up the mission station, but we did so with the hope in our hearts that one day soon we would have the pleasure of opening it again.

THE BEGINNING OF
THE END OF MISSION LIFE

Nagle House Convent, Marandellas,
and St Therese's Mission, Chiduku

1978-1981

Sister Ancilla returned to Nagle House Convent where the Superior, Sister Maureen, was providing tuition in Commercial subjects to the African students in the school. (When I originally arrived in Rhodesia, schools were segregated, but over the years a small percentage of Africans were allowed to be educated in white schools). At the time of my arrival at the convent, there wasn't a Sister qualified to teach Commercial subjects, so Sister Maureen had to employ a secular teacher which was proving costly. She was aware that I had been teaching typing at Mount Melleray, so she requested me to go to Ireland and take a six-month course at McNamara's College in Limerick city that would qualify me to teach the subject at Nagle House school.

I left almost immediately and flew to Shannon where I was met by my sister Eileen and her husband, Jimmy. It was lovely seeing them and all the other family members, but I missed my parents and home desperately. I was assigned to the Presentation Convent in Sexton Street in Limerick for the duration of the course. The Sisters were very welcoming there and, as the college wasn't too far, I was able to take my lunch at the convent daily. At weekends I would often stay with a family member. I didn't find the course too difficult as I already had some experience of typing and teaching and I was successful in my exam at the end of the six months. Before returning to Rhodesia, I spent a few days with the family before flying back to Nagle House.

Shortly after my return, I took on the task of teaching Commercial subjects to African students, and I really enjoyed this work as the girls were so enthusiastic to learn. I gave them books to read to improve their English and requested a synopsis of their work at the weekend. During this time the war was still raging. While I loved the teaching, my heart was with the patients that I had to leave, and I longed for the day when we would experience peace once more and I could return to my work as a nurse in Mount Melleray Mission.

For a long time the government was misleading people into believing that its forces were winning the war. However, in 1979 Margaret Thatcher became prime minister in Britain, and it was decided that a new constitution would have to be satisfactory to Britain and be ratified in free elections. On September 10th, 1979, delegates met at Lancaster House in

London to draw up a constitution and after fourteen weeks of negotiating, the Lancaster House Agreement was signed. On March 4th, 1980, a tightly-monitored election took place, where Robert Mugabe was victorious. A new government was formed and Robert Mugabe was installed as the prime minister on April 18th, 1980. He was the first African to hold that position and in 1980 Rhodesia was renamed Zimbabwe, after the Great Zimbabwe monument.

Many problems awaited both the Church and the new Mugabe government. The initial challenge that faced the Church was to visit each mission station to assess the extent of the damage caused by the war. It was discovered that many of the stations had been razed to the ground, while the others were very badly damaged. Large sums of money would be required to rebuild the mission stations and, following the war, the number of religious priests and nuns was greatly decreased. The political experience and all the events that had taken place during those five years of brutal war had tremendous repercussions on the lives of the people. They were confused as to whether Zimbabwe was going to be a Marxist/Leninist-type state and whether or not they would be allowed practise their religion. This was partly clarified when the Bishop of Salisbury (now Harare) attended the government inauguration ceremony and, speaking to a large gathering of people from different religions and some from no religion, he encouraged them to continue in the practice of their faith.

People were affected emotionally and psychologically by the war experience, and they also experienced a degree of uncertainty and apprehension for the future, not only for themselves but for future generations. From what we were experiencing, a political philosophy was being initiated by the new government which invited people to turn more to the State and less to the reality of God in their lives. All these developments meant that the Church had tremendous problems to deal with, but history shows that it coped as best it could with the unfolding situation. Later on, in 1983, during a speech made in Maynooth while on a visit to Ireland, President Mugabe expressed thanks to the missionaries, and especially to those who lived and struggled along the eastern border of Mozambique, as they had suffered more than anybody else during the war; I can certainly concur with that statement.

Now that the country was considered reasonably safe, I decided to take a trip to Mount Melleray to see for myself how it had fared, and thinking that I would soon be returning to open it again. What wishful thinking that was! As I drove up the driveway, the first thing I noticed was the older section of the convent had dried blood all over its walls. It was a horrible sight. A lot of damage had been done, both to the convent and the church. At the hospital I spoke with a man who told me of his narrow escape. One day, he and his tiny baby were walking up our driveway when he heard the security forces' trucks coming. His only escape was to get right into the middle of the box hedge which lined the driveway. As the soldiers marched about the place, the baby never made a sound. The man said that the baby, sensing its father's great fear, remained silent and, consequently, they both escaped, thank God.

The time had come for the Order Superiors to decide where they were going to open a convent, and I was certain that they were going to return to Mount Melleray where the pioneer Sisters had lived and worked under all kinds of difficult conditions over four decades. They had built the convent, the school and the hospital to very high standards, and those of us who were faced with having to close it during the war took it for granted that we would be returning. This didn't happen, however, and instead the Presentation Sisters exchanged places with Dutch Sisters who had occupied St Therese's Mission in Chiduku, near the town of Rusape. The Superior for the Presentation Order in Zimbabwe thought that the order would have more scope for teaching at the schools in Chiduku than at Mount Melleray.

Sister Aletha and I had to fulfill our duty to obedience and so we moved from Nagle House to Chiduku. At first we had to buy furniture and other commodities to build up the place. I recall that one day the Superior gave me a cheque book to buy necessities, but I returned it unused since I was not in the habit of spending money, and didn't know what to do with a blank cheque book; the Superior was amused. Eventually we managed to get some of the necessities for the convent and the hospital, both of which had been badly damaged. It was extremely difficult to get people to do the work, and fitting windows and doors, repairing toilets and such things was mostly done by the priests as skilled labour was not available at that time. Nevertheless, Sister Aletha and I had an early start each morning. We were very enthusiastic and anxious to help the sick and the wounded

*Judy and Margaret celebrate a birthday in
Tarbert, Co Kerry, in the early 1990s.*

*Sister Eileen and Margaret in the convent chapel at Presentation
Convent, Listowel, Co Kerry, at the final Mass on August 26th, 2007.*

Margaret and Bill in the convent chapel at Presentation Convent, Listowel, Co Kerry, at the final Mass on August 26th, 2007.

Margaret with friends, including Roger (second right), on her visit to Zimbabwe in 1999.

Margaret pictured outside Muture, standing at the memorial plaque to those religious who were murdered at their home during the late 1980s.

*Margaret outside the church at Mount Melleray Mission
on her visit to Zimbabwe in 1999.*

and, above all, the babies; my thoughts were always with the babies since we had left them.

A few days after we arrived at Chiduku, a couple came to the hospital with a very sick baby. They had had triplets but, sadly, two of them had died of malnutrition, and the third baby was badly dehydrated. I decided that I would look after the baby myself and feed it hourly. I had the little packs with all the nutrition required and, with constant care, the baby got to 5lbs. When the time came for the baby to go home, the parents were so very grateful that they put a five dollar note in the baby's little hand to give to me as they were leaving. It would have hurt them had I not taken it. We loved the work and soon made arrangements to set up outlying stations as we had done at Mount Melleray.

The government insisted that each mission be controlled by a qualified nurse, so in this situation I was the one to fill the gap. I had studied for three years to obtain an SRN certificate and one year to obtain a midwifery certificate. I didn't feel I was depriving anyone of their rights, but I always got the feeling that the senior nurse, who was African and who had been at the station throughout the war, resented that I was put in a position above her as an SRN. In spite of that, there seemed to be a pleasant atmosphere in the hospital. Each one had their share of the work; a couple of the African nurses had worked there prior to the war and all were willing to do night duty in turn. I insisted on a sterile pack being prepared for each new patient and the hospital was kept very clean.

We experienced some very pleasant occasions and others that were not pleasant. I recall one Sunday afternoon when the

Sisters from Nagle House Convent decided to pay us a visit. Those occasions were always a joy, but this one in particular was just wonderful. When the Sisters arrived I happened to have a patient in labour and knew she would have her baby in a short time. I ran to the convent to tell the Sisters and ask if anybody would like to see a new baby coming into the world. They came along and one Sister was particularly thrilled by the whole experience. I showed her how to wrap the baby girl in a warm blanket. The very fact of holding that baby in her arms seemed to transform her; she went and sat by the mother occasionally and allowed her to take a peep at her baby every so often. The mother understood perfectly and told the Sister that she would call the baby after her. It was soon time for the Sisters to leave and Sister said she would be back again to see her baby. When she did return, however, the mother and baby were gone back to their village, so the Sister never again got to see the baby who was called after her.

The unpleasant experience was soon to follow. Fr Liam was the priest in charge of the hospital and he was a very saintly man who was always ready to help us. His help was very welcome when a difficult maternity case arrived late at night and a Caesarean section was needed. He would move the patient to the hospital in Nyanga town with either Sister Aletha or myself accompanying the patient. I recall one night when I was alone in the convent when Sister Aletha had gone to Harare for a night. Having worked hard all day, I didn't find time to say the evening prayer until late. As I sat up in bed, reading my prayers by candlelight, I heard the convent door handle being turned.

This happened a couple of times and I was very frightened. I put the candle out and lay quietly there, but sleep was gone for the night.

I told Fr Liam and Sister Aletha when they returned. I was so glad to see them and they expressed great surprise at what had happened, but all went well again for some time. On the next occasion, Sister Aletha stayed at Chiduku while I went to Harare for a night. In fact, we had almost forgotten my experience at this stage. Sister Aletha had gone to bed and was asleep when she was awakened by the sound of the convent door handle being turned. Like me, she too had a sleepless night and spent hours wondering who was up to such mischief. We then decided that in future we would go together to Harare and Fr Liam insisted that we should not stay alone. Little did we know that there was much worse to follow.

We continued our work with even greater enthusiasm because the numbers of patients were increasing as news of our arrival was getting to some very remote spots. At this stage we were attending outside clinics, which covered a very large area, three times a week. The babies were getting vaccinated, records were being kept, and ante-natal records were being carefully filed. All patients at the outlying clinics were checked carefully as we were concerned that all pregnant women attend for ante-natal assessment. Out in rural areas, pelvic assessment was terribly important as the distance from a large hospital could prove dangerous if the mother had a small pelvis and was unable to deliver on her own. In such situations surgery was necessary.

But the people who were carrying out acts like turning the convent doors at night were not interested in either our work or the people we were helping. The next nasty incident happened on Christmas Eve. Poor Fr Liam had spent most of the day preparing the church for Christmas Mass. We helped with flower decorations, laying the altar and other chores. A large number of the population gathered for the Mass and as it started, a group of men walked into the church, talking and laughing as they walked towards the altar. They were most disrespectful to Fr Liam with their singing and loud talk and laughter. We were worried for the priest, and prayed that he would be safe and that he would be able to get Mass completed. Thankfully they left when they thought they had enough damage done. After Mass the priest spoke with members of the congregation that he knew very well. They didn't know any of the men and had never seen them before. At the convent, Fr Liam, Sr Aletha and I spoke for hours, trying to figure out who these people were, and why they were trying to intimidate us.

It was bad enough to have gone through a brutal war where numerous lives had been taken needlessly, and where we and others had experienced the horrible sight of dead bodies thrown on the ground at police stations, with blood pouring from some. Another horrific memory I had was of an occasion at one mission where a tiny baby was kicked about the yard just as a football would be kicked. These memories were still very vivid in our minds, but we thought that now the war was officially over, we would have peace. Not so in our case, as we were about to undergo a night of absolute terror.

Fr Liam had been told to attend a course in Mutare with all the other priests in the region, so Sr Aletha and I were alone in the convent at Chiduku. After another hard day's work, we sat in our sitting room as we did every night. It was January 7th, 1981, and we left the front door open as it was warm weather, but soon we were visited by a bat. Not caring for his company, we moved our tilly lamp to a different position as the bat was attracted to it. When we got him out, we locked our glass door and replaced our tilly lamp to its place on the mantelpiece. Sister Aletha was knitting and I was getting my Christmas cards sorted out when we heard a gentle knock on our glass door. Sister Aletha got up to answer the call when, on some intuition, I told her not to open the door. I knew it was not the ordinary knock to which we were accustomed from the hospital.

The convent was a long low building and Sister Aletha walked to the first bedroom. Being a Shona person herself and therefore fluent in the language, she politely asked who was there. The reply came in a rough, loud voice, "Come outside or we'll fire shots and grenades". Sister Aletha ran back to me to relay the message. I grabbed my torch and cards and we both ran into the only toilet with a lock on the door. We were absolutely terrified and certain they would break in and shoot us. We heard steps running around the convent. They may have thought we had gone outside to make our escape, but we had no place to go and anyway it was far too dangerous. We didn't have a telephone or any way of communicating with anybody to get help. We knew our best help was to turn to the Lord and Our Lady. Strangely enough, on that very day I had

hung a picture of Our Lady just inside the glass door. That
picture was one of the very few items that had remained intact
in the Chiduku convent during the war. I have no doubt but
Our Lady had a hand in saving us on that horrible night.

Sister Aletha and I stood there the entire night, terrified to
make a sound. Occasionally we could hear footsteps and each
time we did, we whispered to each other that this was it. As on
previous occasions, the thought of being shot was not my greatest
fear. I had known of many missionaries who were tortured, some
of whom were beaten to death and some who were shot. To be
shot would be fast, at least. We said many an Act of Contrition
and many prayers to Our Lady during that long night. As the
hours passed by, we whispered to each other and wondered how
we could make our escape. We didn't know where the would-
be intruders were and whether, if we did try to get out as far
the ambulance, they would stop us on the road. I kept telling
Sister Aletha that Our Lady would save us. Eventually we heard
the welcome sound of the dawn chorus and, some time later,
we decided we would try to make our escape. Very gently we
unlocked the toilet door and saw, to our amazement, that the
tilly lamp was still alight on the mantelpiece.

Our movements were very quiet as we quenched the tilly
lamp and I got the key to the ambulance and our handbags.
We decided to face the long and dangerous road to the nearest
town, Rusape. Once safely in the ambulance and without
seeing anybody, we set off on the dangerous road. It took
about an hour to get to Rusape where we hoped that the priest
would be there to take us in, but he, like all the other priests,

had gone to Mutare on retreat. This disappointed us greatly and we decided to go to the local hotel, but, it being so early, the hotel was not yet open. We were so anxious to get to some safe place and eventually the hotel opened. Fortunately for us it was one of the few multi-racial hotels in the country, so Sister Aletha had no problem being served there and we ordered a cup of much-needed coffee. It was still too early to phone Mutare and we thought we should give the priests time to get up. At about seven o'clock we rang the retreat house and when Fr Liam heard my voice, he immediately knew that we were in some trouble.

When they heard the story, he and Bishop Mutume decided to come to our aid without delay. It was wonderful when they arrived and we were able to get into the priest's house and feel safe again. We hadn't felt safe in the hotel as we thought we were being followed. We were grateful that we hadn't been murdered the previous night. I had a clear memory of a night during the war in the German Musame mission, when the priests and some elderly Sisters were taken out and shot. In our current situation the priests felt that perhaps the tilly lamp may have misled the intruders somewhat, as they might not have seen one before and therefore wouldn't have known what it was. They may even have thought that we had some ammunition in the house.

We chatted with Fr Liam and the bishop for some time and they insisted on going out to Chiduku to investigate things for themselves. Sister Aletha and I remained in Rusape in the priest's house and when they returned they said they hadn't seen anything out of the ordinary and that we should go back again. Both Sister Aletha and I were upset and worried. We thought that to ask us to go back into the same situation was unwise and, of course, we were right. Sister Aletha said she would go only under certain circumstances. Firstly, that Fr Liam would stay at the convent with his car parked outside the door. Secondly, that he should accompany us on calls to the hospital. He agreed to do all that and Fr Collier, the priest in Rusape, saw us off and wished us good luck – we needed it all.

As we drove off, we prayed and then filled Fr Liam in on the details of the previous night's happenings. He had not forgotten our Christmas night in the church and the threatening behavior of the group of men. As we arrived at the mission in Chiduku, all seemed quiet and peaceful. The first thing I did was go to the church on my own to thank the Lord for saving us the previous night. I then prepared a room for Fr Liam and got some supper ready. We were about to sit down when a girl who worked for us in the convent came running in and said that they were some men coming through the bushes at the back of the convent. Fr Liam went to look and saw that they were armed with something, though he did not know exactly what. All three of us made a rush for the car. It was a small VW car and I got into the back seat and prayed that the car would start as very often it did not start at the first attempt. Thankfully, on this occasion, it did. As before, we wondered if we were being followed. At one stage Fr Liam asked me if we were on the right road. He had lived in Chiduku for three years prior to the war but was very nervous and wanted to make sure that we were on the road to Rusape again.

The journey seemed endless but, finally, we saw the lights of Rusape and what a joy that was! We were delighted that we would be in a safe place once again. Fr Collier saw the lights of our car from a distance and knew that we must be in trouble again. When we reached his house he came out and put his arms around Sister Aletha and myself and tried to console us. The stress and strain of the journey, plus the fear of the previous night, had taken its toll on us. Fr Collier gave us a meal and prepared rooms for us, which were most welcome. We were lucky to be with one of the kindest priests in the entire area. Sister Aletha and I went to bed, but neither of us could sleep as we could not shake off the feeling of being followed. The Sisters from Harare were informed of what had taken place and they came to visit us the next day. They were extremely sorry for us and we were sorry too, as the realisation dawned that the mission station at Chiduku was no longer safe and that we would have to leave.

Suddenly, I had to think about my future, and what I was going to do; all the nursing stations in the region were closed and the only other thing I could do now was teach typing, but the Commercial school at Nagle House was also closed. Sister Aletha and I left Fr Collier's house in Rusape and went to St Michael's Convent near Harare, where I had lived when I first came to the country more than 25 years earlier. Although I was badly traumatised by the events at Chiduku, I didn't want to return to Ireland as I felt I had no base and no purpose there. I didn't want to work in a big hospital at home, doing work that was ably done by lay people.

In hindsight, I sometimes wonder why I didn't consider re-opening the Commercial school which had proved such a success, especially as there was a growing demand for typing, as well as other skills, at this time. But all the opinion at St Michael's seemed to be in favour of me returning to Ireland. It may have been from a charitable point of view, because they felt I was in need of a holiday. A few weeks later, during which time I began to realise the full trauma of what I had gone through, I decided, along with the Sisters, that I would return to Ireland. I bought a return ticket in the belief that I would be coming back to Zimbabwe sometime in the future.

RETURN TO IRELAND

1981

I travelled to England in March 1981 and stayed at the Presentation Convent in Matlock in Derbyshire for a week. The dark sky and the bare trees, with no flowers and no sunshine, was a huge contrast to what I had left behind in Zimbabwe. What I missed terribly were the night sounds, the wandering hyenas with their peculiar call, the busy crickets and, most of all, the distant sound of the drum beating under the night sky which I had grown to love. After a short break in Matlock, where the Sisters were full of kindness and understanding, I left for home. My parents were long since gone from this world but I was lucky to have a lovely brother, two sisters, two brothers-in-law and a number of nieces and nephews. Their kindness on my return was unforgettable. I stayed with different members of the family for periods of time and they were all great, but I often wondered if I was a burden on them as their children were young at that stage.

I spoke with the Superior General of the Presentation Order on a number of occasions during my first months at home and expressed my desire to work with the less well off, as other congregations were doing. In this way I would be doing work similar to what I had done in Zimbabwe. The Superior General suggested going to the Philippines but I couldn't face the heat there; she also suggested Zambia but I just didn't feel up to it – I could not face another new country, with a new culture and new language. I struggled on for a little longer hoping that somebody would come up with something suitable. Nobody seemed to be aware of what the war in Zimbabwe was like, or of the effect it might have had on me, and so no assistance was offered. Other returned missionaries were in a similar condition, but post-traumatic stress was not a term used in those days. The Superior had been to Zimbabwe during the war and was well aware of how cruel it was. She also knew that I had stood my ground and refused to leave the mission and the hospital, and was prepared to stay on my own and face the gun. I thought that a little bit of consideration for what I had been through would not have gone astray.

I could have gone into a hospital, as I registered with An Bord Altranis when I arrived in Ireland, but that was not what I wanted, as I felt there were lots of people to do that work. Eventually I came across an article about an institution in Athy, County Kildare, which catered for people with addiction problems. I rang the centre and told them that I was interested in doing some work there; they told me to come to Athy, which I did, travelling by train, and I was met at the station by someone from the centre. I didn't discuss wages, work conditions or holidays and, as a result, I didn't get a standard work contract. It was assumed that I would work in a voluntary capacity because I was a nun, receiving bed and board only. I didn't know any better. In Zimbabwe I had been paid fully and that had been the situation since I first completed nurses' training. Back in Ireland, the Presentation Sisters gave me the same pocket money that all Sisters received and my family had to come and collect me and take me back when I had a break.

I liked the work and admired all that had been done since the place opened. It certainly was a new experience but I didn't have training for it and I had to depend on my own good sense. I felt deeply for the people there and for their families, and I did what I could to help them. While there, I learned that the greatest suffering in life is to have no one to love you. Some people had no one to visit them, even to send a Christmas card, and the staff did their best to compensate for that in many thoughtful ways. I knew one gentleman whose daughter died in a fire due to his drinking. His suffering was indescribable. He had longed to see a member of his family, but nobody ever came. Eventually he got ill and died and I could not believe it when I saw his wife and other members of his family, not only at the funeral, but actually crying. If only they had an idea of how he had suffered; he was such a lonely man during all those years. There were many such cases and all I could do was listen in silence as they shared their burden of regret.

As time went on I found myself getting very tired, I was getting frequent colds and had lost my voice. I arranged a meeting with the Order Superior where I made her aware of how I was feeling and asked her if I could have a base, a place in some convent, instead of constantly calling on members of my own family. A few days later she sent word that I could go to Presentation Convent in Listowel, County Kerry. This was near one of my sisters and my brother, and my other sister who was always taking care of me was not far away either.

I left Athy and moved to Listowel in 1983 where, at last, I had some independence and a place to put my belongings. As time went on I longed more and more for my beloved Zimbabwe, and I found it extremely difficult to settle down. While the Sisters were most helpful, they were occupied with running both a primary and a secondary school. There were a few elderly nuns who required care and while I gave a hand looking after them, there were lay staff employed to do that.

A short time later I was asked to work in Bruree, County Limerick – another rehabilitation centre similar to the one in Athy, and run by the same organisation. I worked hard there and being a resident nurse was quite demanding. As in Athy, there were lay staff on set hours by day and by night, nevertheless, the call of "Sister Margaret to reception" rang loud and clear very frequently. Bruree is some distance from the city, but the intake of people with addiction problems came from all over. The centre is set in a large old building on what was once a thriving farm and the grounds were ideal for those in recovery as they provided both physical and mental therapy. The men in recovery were trained in building, woodwork, gardening and growing vegetables, while the women benefited by learning various skills and being involved in keeping the centre in good order. Various specialists were employed to help in the recovery process and it was good to see the people go back into the mainstream of society with a more positive attitude.

During this time I went to Listowel convent occasionally for a break and the Sisters there helped me greatly. My driving licence was no longer valid and I had to sit the driving test. The Sisters in Listowel kindly allowed me to use their car for practice and arranged that I could have a few lessons before doing the test. I was a bit rusty as I hadn't driven since that night of terror in Chiduku. When the time came for me to undergo the test, a Sister accompanied me to the driving test centre in Tralee and while I underwent the test, she very kindly prayed in the church. All prayers were heard as I passed first time. I was delighted and very grateful to the Sisters. When it came to holiday time, the Sisters didn't forget me either. They took two weeks annually at their magnificent resort at Ballinskelligs, County Kerry. I was invited and, while I had heard of the place, I had no knowledge of its immense beauty. The journey itself was very interesting as the scenery in that area is breathtaking, and the Sisters had prepared a delicious picnic which we enjoyed, sitting on the beach in Glenbeigh.

When we arrived at the holiday house we were welcomed by the Sister in charge, Sister Vianney, who was a wonderful person, full of consideration and kindness. I soon discovered that, like me, Sister Vianney was from Athea, my hometown. There was an immediate bond between us and we loved discussing old times, places, dancehalls and other subjects of parochial interest that mean so much to people who are away from their place of birth for a long time. There were lots of things for me to enjoy, things I hadn't seen or done for years. On my first few days we went picking periwinkles which we cooked and ate. The Sisters had a meadow and when I saw the men saving hay at the back of the holiday house, it reminded me so much of home. A few of us even went out to help; I always loved the smell of hay and this was an opportunity I never expected to find again. Having been away from home and the farm since I was 15 years old, it meant so much to me to be in a meadow again, with the scent of the hay and the rhythm of the work around me.

We had other great outings, but the most spectacular was our day out at sea at Skellig Michael – that really was a day to remember. My friends and I set out early by boat and away we went in brilliant sunshine, the sea was calm and, to my amazement, some gannets and puffins came so close to the boat, I felt they were almost within reach. In the distance we saw a huge snow-white rock. Drawing closer, the chatter of the gannets as they were nestling into every possible crevice was intriguing – they were making sure that nobody invaded their territory as this was the 'gannet rock'. On we sailed towards Skellig Michael itself, situated far out in the Atlantic Ocean. On arrival, we took a walk around this amazing place before settling down to one of the delicious picnics which only the nuns can make. We climbed the steps to see the beds used by the monks when they lived here, and I thought how cold and uncomfortable they must have been.

Each day at Ballinskelligs brought something new and exciting. Apart from swimming, we walked out as far as possible on the beach to visit each little island. One afternoon, my friend, Sister Eileen, and I got marooned on one of those islands as the sea came in very fast. Nobody knew where we were so we had no choice but to wait until the tide went out again. Our holiday went all too fast and eventually the time came to bid farewell to the place and to thank our lovely, kind host, Sister Vianney, for her tremendous kindness in making our stay a most enjoyable one.

After that trip I went back to Bruree to continue my work there. On my return I noticed some new faces. People were leaving when their course was completed and new people were replacing them and it gave me great satisfaction to see people looking happy again. The illness of drug addiction and alcoholism brought nothing to people's lives but misery, unhappiness and family divisions. Just to see one smiling face was always a treat and a reward for one's efforts. Because I had no formal training before taking up this appointment, trying to talk to people and to give advice was difficult, so I just fell back on my own common sense and judgment again. The various experiences of my own life proved helpful occasionally.

I heard that a course on drug addiction was being held in Coolmine Drug Centre in Dublin and I was asked if I would be interested in being a participant. Non-drug-addicted people were allowed to attend provided they partook fully in the course which was one month long. Fortunately for me, there was another nun equally interested, so we decided to go ahead and do it. While it was most interesting, it was very difficult and demanding and really tested participants' strength of character. The entire centre had to be kept spotlessly clean, with each person's room being inspected daily. One's hairbrush, comb and toothbrush were inspected and if all was not in order, then a correction was made and everything had to be put right.

What struck me very forcefully during this course was how anxious people with addictions were to rid themselves of this malice. Addiction was the scourge that had taken control and was destroying, not only their lives, but also the lives of those closest to them. Some participants were friendly and anxious to share their problems, both in the group sessions and privately. Their stories were distressing but now that they were getting counselling and help they were hopeful of recovery. Anybody who stepped out of line in the course was punished and each one of us had to become involved in the correction method. Occasionally this would necessitate the use of harsh language and what I regard as street language. I disliked having to do that as I detest bad language, but it was necessary in this situation. Everything was done for the benefit of those who had fallen into, or were snared into, the miserable life of drug addiction. My Sister companion and I were glad to have undertaken the course, and we felt we gained a lot from it that would guide us along the way in helping other people to improve their quality of life. When I returned to work in Bruree I felt a bit more confident now that I had completed some formal addiction training.

As time passed, I got to know the residents well, and some better than others. Nobody ever refused to do things for me around the centre and I found them more than willing to give a helping hand when necessary. There was one man who called to the centre frequently, either to visit a patient that he knew or to help out. He was a very kind gentleman and would willingly go to the village of Bruree when I needed something or just to post a letter. All these things were helpful to me since I didn't have a car. Often this man would have a bar of chocolate in his pocket for me, which I found so thoughtful. Another person who called frequently was Fr O'Callaghan from Millstreet in County Cork. He had a keen interest in each patient and he would join us occasionally in the duty room for a cup of tea. I got to know him quite well as he would often stay on and join us for the Rosary.

On one occasion I mentioned to Fr O'Callaghan about a conversation I had had with a Sister in one of the convents. Sister had mentioned that many of the convents would be closing sometime soon. In fact, she said that many had closed already. Naturally I wondered where the Sisters would reside if that should happen and who would support them. Her answers were vague and she was uncertain and apprehensive. She asked me what provision I could make for myself in such circumstances. Without Sister realising it, I was absolutely shocked at what she said. I had no idea whatsoever about such uncertainties, having lived all my life under the umbrella of authority.

With the deaths of both my parents, I no longer had a place I could really call home. Already I had imposed on my sisters and brother for six months while waiting for Superiors to get me the type of employment I wanted. They were still insisting that it was too soon for me to return to Zimbabwe, but yet nothing really suitable was provided for me and, as a result, I felt that I was in a sort of a limbo situation. Fr O'Callaghan listened very carefully to everything I had to say. He explained about the shortage of vocations and said there were a lot of nuns retiring, adding that it was inevitable that some changes would have to be made. He had heard that convents were closing as they could no longer be maintained.

In the months following these revelations, I began, finally, to think about myself and my future. One night the thought struck me that maybe I had done my bit for others and that now it was time for me to consider the type of future I might embark upon without others making the decisions for me. But I was, after all, without a home, a car or a salary, so how could I possibly make a living? Above all, I was asking myself, what of my commitment to the Lord and would He understand? I began to consider leaving religious life altogether because the changes in that life seemed to be full of uncertainty and I couldn't see any future for myself as a nun in Ireland. Pondering on the unknown can be a daunting experience at the best of times. Someone who has never been free from dependence on Superiors for guidance on practically every issue of daily living is even more likely to suffer from uncertainty when that dependence is removed.

On Fr O'Callaghan's next visit to the centre, I broached the subject with him. He appeared to be shocked that I should be thinking of leaving the convent. I asked him why he was so shocked since so many others were leaving or had already left. He replied, saying that he thought my work in Bruree was having an effect on many people and it appeared that they appreciated my efforts. Weeks passed and on his next visit he was anxious to know how I felt and asked if I was reading the Bible. My assurance convinced him that I had prayed and asked for guidance. I had not changed my mind, but instead had become more determined. Surprisingly, Fr O'Callaghan told me that if I wanted to leave he could get me a good nursing job, the type of work I had requested. An elderly lady he knew had suffered a slight stroke but had made a good recovery and was anxious to return home from hospital. Her husband had died a few years previously and, without a family of her own, she was in need of somebody who could stay full-time with her. His advice to me was to give the idea some thought and to let him know my decision when he would call again.

Making a decision of this magnitude was going to be traumatic and stressful for me. Having gone through six years of a horrific war, escaping bombs and landmines on many occasions, I asked myself if I would be able to endure much more. I felt that the work in Athy and Bruree was far from suitable for my health at that stage, having come from a war situation and, particularly, without specialised training. Taking all things into consideration I became more convinced that this decision was the right one, but such a change would be a huge decision for me and I needed help and guidance. My good friend, Sister Eileen, came to my assistance and helped me in making my final decision. Her words to me were, "Since you feel so strongly about your decision, it must be God's will that you follow it". This gave me great encouragement and peace of mind and, with her help, we got started on procedures. Firstly, I had to inform the Regional Superior, Sister Mary, that I was leaving. Her response was one of utter shock and she, in turn, had to inform the Superior of the congregation in Monasterevin in County Kildare.

I got a phone call from the congregation Superior requesting that I visit her immediately. I think she was convinced that she would get me to change my mind. When we met, she seemed to be quite upset and told me it was a terrible shock for her and for the congregation. She asked me a number of times why was I leaving and I told her that I just wanted to be myself. I asked her if she would request a dispensation from vows from Rome and eventually she said she would. She told me that I would also have to write to Rome and give my reasons for leaving. As expected, she was worried about my future, but I assured her that I had secured a suitable job nursing an elderly lady in her own home. I explained that this meant that I would have a place to live and weekly wages and she seemed to be happy with that situation.

The next big step for me was to tell my family. My sister Bridie was the first to be told. She was very understanding and compassionate and didn't make a fuss; in fact, she praised all my efforts over the years and said she would assist me in every way possible. I subsequently informed my brother Pa and my sister Eileen. They didn't put any obstacle in my way either and were happy that I had managed to get a suitable job. I then informed the staff at Bruree and they wished me the best of luck.

After a short break, Sister Eileen accompanied me to Cork to meet Mrs Graves, the woman who needed nursing care, to discuss job arrangements and to consider my suitability to care for her. She was a lovely person and anxious that I should take up the position as soon as possible. I assured her that I would do everything possible to help her overcome the effects of the mild stroke she had suffered and we were both happy with the outcome of the interview. By this time all the convent Superiors had been informed of my decision to leave religious life. There was now little more for me to do other than to collect the few items of clothing which I had brought back from Zimbabwe from the convent in Sexton Street in Limerick, where I had transferred from Listowel. That was a painful moment and I shed a few tears when walking out the convent gates for the very last time. I looked back and gave a final wave to the Sisters.

A NEW JOURNEY BEGINS

County Cork and County Kerry

1985-1998

The feeling of depending on myself for the first time ever, even with some help from on high, was very frightening. However, a warm welcome awaited me, both from Mrs Graves and the woman I was taking over from. She very kindly stayed on for the first night to get me initiated into the required treatments for Mrs Graves. As soon as we were on our own, Mrs Graves and I gradually got to know each other. She was happy to be out of hospital and looked after in her own home by a qualified nurse. Mrs Graves had a few chores she wished me to carry out – number one was to take her dog for a daily walk on the strand in Shanagarry. What a joy! I shall never forget how happy I suddenly felt with the lead in hand, a happy dog and myself walking along the beautiful beach. The next request was, equally, a huge surprise; Mrs Graves asked if I would drive her lovely automatic car when necessary. The Lord was taking care of me. All of a sudden I had a home, a job, weekly wages and now the use of a car – surely I could not ask for more.

A date was arranged for me to meet with the Presentation Order Provinicial Superior, Sister Mary, and this meeting took place at a hotel in Midleton, County Cork. There were a couple of forms to be signed by both of us, and Sister Mary had also been asked to give me some money by the Superior General, just to get me started in my new life. After having a cup of coffee I took Sister Mary to show her where my patient lived. The house and the grounds looked wonderful and Sister Mary was very happy to see that I was already settled in my new life and surroundings.

Friends of Mrs Graves had arranged that I would have two nights off every couple of weeks. Once more luck came my way when I happened to meet the then parish priest, Fr Troy. I told him who I was and explained my situation to him. He told me that he knew where there was a lovely little house, situated high above the cliffs at Ballycotton, directly across from the lighthouse and looking out on the Atlantic. The rent on the house was minimal and how I looked forward to my first and many subsequent visits there. On one memorable occasion my sister Bridie, her daughters, Catherine and Sarah, and baby Danny, who was just ten months old, arrived and stayed for the weekend. They were amazed at the outstanding beauty of Ballycotton. That particular visit is still spoken about as we had such fun and we went for early morning walks up the cliffs in lovely sunshine. The lighthouse was a great attraction and fresh fish, straight out of the sea, was simply delicious. Needless to say, they were reluctant to leave and I was equally sad to see them go.

Mrs Graves and I were getting on very nicely and she was beginning to walk with the help of a tripod. Always a very keen gardener, as was her late husband, Arthur, she enjoyed many hours of peace and quiet sitting outside, either reading, which was one of her favourite hobbies, or just admiring the work that they both had put into making a colourful and well-manicured garden. Each day brought Mrs Graves a little step further on her path towards recovery. I saw her smile much more frequently, happy to be in her own surroundings again. Each week she would accompany me to Midleton to buy the groceries – she knew the stores and would guide me to the different places and after lunch on Sundays we would go for a drive to one of her favourite places. Mrs Graves had a sister, Alice, who lived in Fermanagh, and she loved to come and spend some time with us. It was great to hear them chat away and reminisce on former times. Her nieces and nephews were also frequent visitors and she loved having them as she enjoyed their stories and anecdotes. Gradually I got to know them all and always enjoyed their company.

After my weekend breaks, it was always a joy getting back to work with Mrs Graves. She loved having me back again and into our usual routine. I thought her walking was improving and her speech, which had been slightly affected, was by now almost perfect. The physiotherapist was most efficient and achieved great results. Mrs Graves and I were now on Christian name terms, at her request, and we could talk to each other and trust each other on all matters. She was called Judy, although her name was Suzanna, and all her great neighbours and wonderful friends used that name.

I had visitors from my former life with Sisters Eileen and Vianney keeping in regular contact. In fact, I got so much correspondence from Zimbabwe that I requested the Regional Superior to keep my address and telephone number private as I just could not cope with the amount of correspondence that was arriving. I became more and more familiar with life outside the convent; we had been told in the novitiate that the world was a bad place, but for me now it was a wonderful place. The freedom to walk or swim or converse with people, to talk when I liked and not to have to listen to bells tolling, was a great freedom. No more answering to Mother for every fiddle-faddle and to be able to read a book of one's own choice was wonderful. For me it was a great place and my freedom was a precious gift.

I liked to visit Cork city and had started to see plays and the occasional film. One particular day remains very vivid in my mind. I was walking along Patrick Street when I met a man who I recognised at first glance. We stopped and I asked if he was the man I used to know in Bruree, the man who always brought me a bar of chocolate when shopping, and sure it was. We chatted for a few minutes and he asked if I would care for a cup of tea. I agreed and found him to be polite and gentlemanly. His name was Bill and he was working with his brother on a farm somewhere near Cork city. He told me he still visited Bruree occasionally to meet his friends. On leaving, he asked where I lived and whether he could pay me a visit sometime. I agreed and gave him my phone number.

A couple of weeks passed and then one day Bill phoned to say he would like to visit me. He came to the house and the three of us, Judy, Bill and I, enjoyed a cup of tea, and he was completely relaxed. Off he went after about an hour saying he would call again sometime soon. Judy remarked on how gentle and kind-looking this young man was. I explained to Judy where and how I had got to know him. Bill became a regular visitor and it amazed me that he kept coming so frequently. On leaving he would always ask if it was all right to call again. In fact, I was now beginning to enjoy his company. In addition, he was what one would call 'tall, dark and handsome', with sparkling brown eyes. I wondered why he hadn't married and he told me that he had experienced love, but had a change of heart in that situation.

Each new visit seemed to bring the two of us closer. While our initial greeting was a warm handshake, our farewells soon turned into a little hug. I was amazed at myself that I didn't show any resistance whatsoever. In fact, it reminded me of former times out in the rural areas of Zimbabwe prior to the war, when we enjoyed some wonderful evenings of friendship and love. It was then and only then that I had my first feeling of love merely by touching another human being while dancing. Now I was having the same feelings once more, as Bill gently hugged me before going home. This added to my happiness and it was obvious that Bill was enjoying his visits.

At night in bed I would ask myself where all of this was leading me. I was fully aware that he was a good deal younger than me but, if it was true love, did it really matter? Bill was anxious to take me out but I would not leave Judy in the house on her own and, in the circumstances, I couldn't ask anybody to sit in with her as nobody knew our situation. We did occasionally go for a walk along the beach which was most enjoyable and gave us an opportunity to talk about our lives. At this stage I needed advice and guidance. Fortunately, I had a niece, Patricia, who was just home from college and I knew I could confide in her. She could appreciate my situation perfectly and strongly advised me to follow my heart. That was a big help. Patricia had been a friend for many years, so I knew I was talking with the right person. Another faithful friend was Sister Eileen, and she had already met Bill at an earlier stage as both visited me at Bruree. I thought her first reaction was a little cautious, but then she began to see things from my perspective and said she would support me all the way.

Finally, one evening, as I was walking on the beach with Bill, with his arm around me, he whispered in my ear, asking if I would marry him. He said his love for me was very great. At first I was shocked and asked Bill if he would give me time to consider the matter. I knew I should tell my great friend Judy and I hoped that she wouldn't be shocked. When I told her I was amazed at her lovely response. Happiness, she said, was a priority for all of us. Of course she asked me not to leave her, and once more I promised that I would never do so. Now that my friends were aware of my intentions and I was assured of their support, the time had come to give Bill an answer. I knew I was taking a huge step and asked myself many times over whether it would work out? I felt that the Lord had taken care of me all through my life and thought that He would continue to do so. Naturally, I prayed about my decision and finally I was ready to give Bill an answer on our next meeting.

Needless to say I didn't have long to wait as Bill was eagerly awaiting and hoping for a successful reply. When I thought the right moment had come, with Bill's lovely brown eyes glued on mine and me wrapped in his arms, I looked up at him and said, "My answer is yes, I will marry you". We hugged and kissed for a long time as Bill was absolutely overcome with joy. He promised he would take such good care of me and that he would love me forever. Today I can honestly say that he always has, and continues to take great care of me in our married life.

The next question was when and where the important event would take place. Neither of us wanted a big wedding – we just wanted to go away some place quietly, so we considered going to Rome. My family were anxious that we should marry in Ireland, but they also understood how we felt. Finally, with the knowledge of both families and especially with the blessing and joy of Bill's lovely mother, we finally settled on Rome. I knew we would not have a problem getting married there as my priest friends with whom I had worked in Zimbabwe knew many companions working in Rome, and in a short time everything was in order.

At home, both families helped with getting suitable clothes for the occasion. My sister Bridie and her daughter Catherine took us shopping. Bill, of course, looked after his outfits but I had worn a nun's habit for all of my adult life, and prior to that my parents had done all my shopping, so I had to depend on my family for guidance as to what was suitable. I was delighted with their choices and felt very grateful for their guidance. My other nieces were in England during this time but all were concerned for our happiness. People were extremely helpful and encouraging. Finally, a date was set for our marriage. While we were both very happy, I was a little nervous, but I prayed a lot and told myself that I would trust in the Lord as I had always done. He had saved me in dangerous situations and perhaps this was a way of rewarding me for my efforts.

Bill and I flew to Rome a few days before the wedding was due to take place. The ceremony, which was conducted by a Carmelite priest, was beautiful and during it a great feeling of happiness and peace came over me. I looked at Bill and his face was radiant. The feeling of unity and love between us both was delightful – the love of another human being is truly a wonderful gift in life. That night we were given the bridal suite in the hotel; I stood for a few moments looking out on the streets on one of the world's most beautiful cities, feeling a sense of perfect peace and happiness.

Our priest friends joined us for breakfast and later helped us exchange our money and directed us towards St. Peter's and many more sights. We had a few days in which to enjoy it all and to purchase some gifts for our very good friends. Soon it was time to say farewell to the great city of Rome which had brought Bill and myself tremendous joy and happiness and an assurance of a happy married life. Back in Ireland, for the remainder of our free time, we toured some of the beauty spots before visiting our relations. Bill's mother and family gave us a huge welcome home and my family had a lovely family gathering with a delicious meal, including cake and champagne.

With all the celebrations over, it was time to go back to work and I was eagerly looking forward to seeing Judy to give her a full account of the entire occasion. Judy had been to Rome on numerous occasions so this made it all the more interesting for both of us. Now that Bill and I were married, Judy invited Bill to stay at her house and we were grateful for this generous invitation. In the meantime we were on the lookout for a house of our own and within the year we bought one in Cloyne, a few miles from Midleton in County Cork. Judy's situation was now to be considered and we discussed with her whether she wished to come with us. Judy knew I would never leave her alone, yet it was a big decision for her and, of course, it needed the input of her sister Alice and her nephews. They talked with Judy and then went to see our new home. They were all happy with it but, most importantly, Judy was happy to come with us. I was delighted, as she loved being with Bill and myself. The three of us settled in Cloyne for the next few years, with me looking after Judy and Bill working in a local factory in Midleton.

A few years later, Bill's job fell through. I was anxious to move nearer to my relations since I was away from them for most of my life and, fortunately, Bill found employment in Tarbert, County Kerry. There too, we found a suitable house for sale and bought it. It was wonderful to be near the family again, including my brother and sisters and their families. Judy was happy with the situation; she loved our house and we gave her the front room which enabled her to gaze out across the green fields where cattle grazed contentedly. What she enjoyed

Sr Francesca O'Donnell, who travelled with Margaret on their original trip to Rhodesia (Zimbabwe) in 1955, pictured with Margaret outside Margaret's home in Tarbert, Co Kerry, in 2000.

Sr Aletha, with whom Margaret worked at St Therese's Mission in Chiduku, pictured with Margaret outside her home in Tarbert, Co Kerry, during a visit to Ireland in 2001.

Sr Aletha, pictured with Bill in Tarbert, Co Kerry, during her visit to Ireland in 2001.

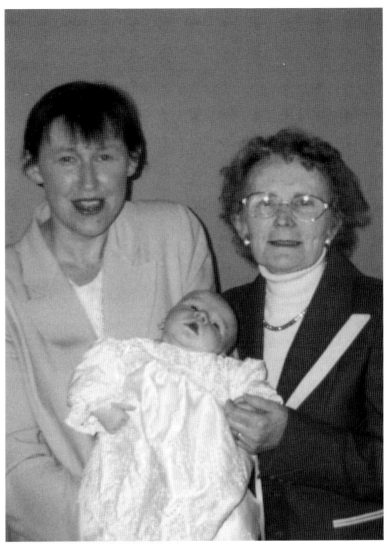

Margaret, pictured with her niece, Sarah Clancy,
and grandnephew, Paddy Joe, on his christening day in 2001.

*Margaret with her sister, Eileen, and niece, Patricia Danaher,
at a family event in Adare, Co Limerick, in 2005.*

Margaret and her sister, Bridie, in 2006.

most of all were the visits of my niece's little children, Danny and Linda, who called regularly. They loved Judy and Judy loved them. Sadly, during this time, Judy lost her sister Alice. This saddened her greatly, as they had enjoyed each other's company so much. Judy's nieces and nephews were extremely kind to her and even though they lived so far away, mostly in the North of Ireland, they visited as often as possible and they all helped to console her in her grief.

Although she was advancing in age, Judy was still an avid reader. She also loved the radio and enjoyed it particularly while having breakfast. Bill always helped me to raise up Judy in bed for breakfast, and also to watch a neighbour's cattle pass by our house when they were returning to the field after having been milked. Life continued very happily for the three of us for a few more years, but when Judy was in her ninety-third year, I began to see her deteriorate. One day when she was sitting by the kitchen fire, she mentioned that she was not fully able to read any more. This, she told me, made her unhappy, as life meant reading and she loved poetry. Gradually she was taking less interest in what was going on around her and the doctor, who knew her so well, recognised the gradual downhill process. I could not bear to think that I would lose Judy. By that time, she and I had had a total of ten wonderful years together.

She went downhill and I became exhausted from looking after her, especially as I used to check on her throughout the night. The doctor insisted that I should have a little time off, as he was concerned about my condition. Judy's nieces very kindly looked after her while Bill and I went away for a week's holiday to Jersey. When we returned we could see a big change in Judy and were told that she had been constantly asking for Bill and me. Finally, one Sunday afternoon in 1993, the doctor and the public health nurse said that Judy was dying and all the family were informed. During my nursing career, I had seen many beautiful deaths but none like Judy's. Bill was due home at 2.30pm and she waited until he arrived. Minutes before that she turned her head slightly and smiled up at me, so I was happy even though my heart was breaking. Bill was just wonderful; he kept telling Judy that we would all be together soon again and she just closed her eyes, looking ever so peaceful. She was laid to rest with her husband Arthur in Cloyne, County Cork.

Now that Judy was gone it meant that our days, and especially mine, changed somewhat. I had more time on my hands and had to decide what way to use it best. There was a self-development course starting in Tarbert and I signed up for it. It was just one week long but I found it very fulfilling. Various speakers came to talk to us about health, exercise, personal security, drug abuse and other subjects. Later on I did a course in adult literacy and got to know Mary Pierce, a woman who has done tremendous work in this field. She kindly gave me a lift from Listowel to Tralee on the course nights, and sometime later asked me if I would be interested in taking on one or two students to help them with reading and writing. I did this for a couple of years and found it very rewarding. I also trained as a Eucharistic minister, which was a great privilege.

Our local parish priest decided that the ministers should take the Holy Communion to the sick and the house-bound and I was very happy to do this. I loved meeting the people as they were always so welcoming and I continued to act as a minister for a good number of years.

ZIMBABWE REVISITED AND TIME FOR REFLECTION

Tarbert, County Kerry

1998-present

Life continued contentedly for Bill and me and one day, while having lunch, we heard the postman drop some mail in the mailbox. I picked it up and on my way back to the table I noticed that there was a letter from Zimbabwe. I proceeded to read its contents and therein was an invitation to go to Zimbabwe to celebrate the fiftieth anniversary of the Presentation Sisters' arrival in what was then known as Rhodesia. 1949 had been the first time the Presentation Sisters even saw any part of Africa, but they had known all about its great needs, its poverty and, in certain areas, its riches. They also knew that there was huge potential for nursing and teaching, and when and where possible to show the people God's love through their actions and words. My reaction to the invitation was one of joy and excitement. I was glad that Bill was there with me to experience my joy. He returned to work and by evening time I had my mind fully made up to accept the invitation, and I knew Bill would encourage me to go and see the people and the country which I loved so much.

In the letter the Sisters informed me that they would take care of me from the moment I arrived at the airport until my departure. Little did I know when I read the letter of invitation that they had a wonderful itinerary arranged for me that incorporated visiting places that have always had a special place in my heart. My first step, however, was to reply to the invitation with gratitude. Then I had to get vaccinations against tropical diseases, in particular against my friends the mosquitoes! Would they bite on this occasion, I wondered? As the weather would be slightly cooler in July, I felt I might escape their punishment and my doctor made sure I was well-protected. Having fixed a departure date and time of flight, packing the suitcase was an easy matter. My niece agreed to take me to Shannon. Now that all the preliminaries were taken care of, I began to concentrate on Zimbabwe. It was eighteen years since I had left. I wondered if the Sisters and all the people I knew had changed much during that long period and if the country I had known so well had been transformed. All would be revealed in a couple of weeks!

In July 1999, I set off from Shannon to London, and on to Frankfurt airport, which was my last stop before arriving in Zimbabwe. It was morning time when the plane started to descend. My eyes were glued to the window and away in the distance I spotted an occasional swimming pool; I wondered if the owners were still enjoying them. Coming closer to ground

I could see tobacco fields and maize with the corn just taking on its golden colour. The pilot informed us that the weather was cool as it was just coming towards the end of the cold season. Finally we arrived on *terra firma*. Looking up at the balcony I was surprised to see large crowds of African people talking and laughing; it wasn't like that the last time I had been here. I spotted two Sisters who were waving furiously at me and I knew then that they were my friends. I recognised Sister Bridget as she had visited me in Tarbert, but I didn't recognise the other Sister until Sister Bridget said, "Don't you know Sister Ancilla?" Sister Ancilla had always been one of my very best friends; it was she who came to stay with me when I was alone during the most dangerous time of the war. Immediately I recognised her face and realised I hadn't known her because her hair had got so grey. Rejoicing and celebrating began immediately and there was great excitement.

On our way to St. Michael's Convent where I had lived for so long, the Sisters began to tell me of the many changes that had taken place over the years. The 'whites only' signs had been removed from all large apartments and the use of the term 'one boy' had also been done away with. But there were many other disagreeable sights which I would soon encounter. Nevertheless, it was a holiday I was given and I was determined to enjoy it. After the long haul from Ireland I was tired. Sister Bridget, who was responsible for my trip, informed me that I would have a couple of hours rest, then lunch, and what was to follow soon dispelled any trace of tiredness. There was a Landrover waiting outside the convent door ready to take me to a new mission station called Guruve, and run by none other than my faithful friend who was so protective of me during our troubled times, Sister Aletha.

The journey to Guruve was most enjoyable, what with the brilliant blue sky, everyplace looking green and fresh and the baboons chasing up and down the rocks with their young on their backs. Higher up on the side of the hill the Sisters spotted a giraffe with its young close by – I was extremely lucky to see the giraffe as I had not been that close before. The welcome and the excitement at my arrival at Guruve were tremendous. As I entered the little convent and looked to my right, there stood a table with a large cake saying 'Welcome Margaret' – that was just the beginning of my ten wonderful days. My few days with Sister Aletha passed all too quickly and it was soon time to get back to Harare to dress up for the big occasion.

The convent chapel was a sight to behold with all the wonderful tropical flowers. Many archbishops, bishops and priests lined the altar. The congregation packing the chapel was a combination of all denominations, colours and creeds. That was a most welcome change and added hugely to the enjoyment of the celebration. The choir was excellent and I felt very privileged to be asked to help in taking the sacred vessels to the altar for Mass. On previous occasions the prime minister would have been invited, but no longer. Mr Mugabe had allowed the country to deteriorate and was no longer welcome. After Mass, we were taken to a very large canteen where delicious food was served to suit all tastes and cultures.

There I met many of my great friends – priests, Sisters and lay people – all of whom welcomed me with open arms. One or two of my former patients were among the crowd and a few of my typists. Incredibly, I actually met the lovely girl who, many years earlier, had presented me with the *huku* (hen). To add to all this joy, a large stand had been erected to display photos taken at events down through the years and I was delighted to be reminded of many of the good times I'd had in the country. This great day ended with many speeches and I was personally thanked by the Provincial Superior for coming out to Zimbabwe to celebrate this very special day.

The next part of my itinerary was a great treat. Sisters Bridget and Ancilla had requested from a friend the use of a holiday house which was situated in one of the most picturesque spots in Zimbabwe. It had excellent views, was a comfortable house and, most importantly, it was a short distance from Mount Melleray Mission, somewhere that has always occupied a special place in my heart. My time was slipping away all too fast and I could only spend three nights in this magnificent setting. The Sisters were anxious to take me to Troutbeck Inn, a lovely hotel which we had visited frequently in earlier times. We knew the family who owned it very well through our schools. Sadly, there were many trips I could not take due to the terrible conditions of the roads which had been totally neglected since Independence. We went on picnics and long walks where we enjoyed and admired the lovely trees, especially the Msasa, which have a lovely amber and wine red colour. I also saw the Flame Lily, which is the national flower of Zimbabwe and is a delightful, delicate flower with deep pink and yellow petals.

Finally the day arrived when I was going to see Mount Melleray Mission. As the road was in such poor condition, the Sisters asked Father O'Regan to do the driving. My heart ached as we stopped for a moment at the home of Mr and Mrs Mee, whom we had found shot and battered to death. Their house now looked deserted and sad. On we went, and I couldn't wait to get my first glimpse of Mount Melleray. The first building to be seen as one enters the mission is the church where we stopped for a moment only, as I told the priest I wanted to visit there on my own later on. We proceeded to the convent which looked much the same, but sadly there was no Mother Peter this time to greet me. She had gone to God in 1983 after a heart attack in Matlock in England.

From there we went to the hospital. It lacked the happy atmosphere that once prevailed. Nonetheless, the African Carmelite Sisters very kindly treated us to afternoon tea which we appreciated. I mentioned to one of the Sisters that I would like to visit the church, and in the goodness of her heart she came along with me. The visit was great but it brought back memories of all the African people who had been killed in the area. For a box of soap or a bag of sugar one could lose one's life, and some did. The hedge where the man hid with his baby when he heard the army coming was still there, and the older part of the convent was still without a ceiling; it reminded me of the day I saw the walls covered in blood. I left Mount Melleray with a heavy heart, but Father O'Regan said he was taking me to World's View, a renowned viewing point in the Eastern Highlands.

This was an amazing place with the wonderful tropical sun at its highest, shining all around us. We sat on the rocks and took the opportunity to enjoy the outstanding panorama. From there we were destined for Mutare, a lovely town situated close to the Mozambique border. Again, we had good friends here, also known through the schools, and it was in Mutare that I saw the biggest changes. I was invited to stay at the bishop's house for a couple of days. During the war this bishop had suffered greatly, mainly because of his colour, and Mother Peter and I had visited him in prison on many occasions, bringing him tea and sandwiches, and now he wanted to thank me.

I was shocked to see so many houses blocked up and surrounded with barbed wire; each house seemed to have an Alsatian dog for protection. The African people were now running the country, and while that in itself was a good thing, there was something radically wrong. The war was over when I left the country in 1981, but now there seemed to be as much fear or even more than during the war. I was not allowed to go any place on my own, not even to the post office to post a few cards. Neither was I allowed to go into Harare city as I was told that it was not safe. I loved Harare as it was the city where I did my SRN training. What came to my mind very clearly were the good old days, when work was finished for the day and off I would go in the evening with my Rosary beads in hand to enjoy the peace and quiet of the bush, to listen to and look at the beautiful African birds. I had frequently slept alone in the convent when my companion went away, but those days were long gone though their memory still lingered.

The bishop gave me a lovely time while in Mutare, taking me to see the famous Vumba mountains. There was one place he insisted that I should see, and that was the site where the wonderful English missionaries had chosen to live towards the end of the war. They had felt fearful when living near our mission at Avila; indeed we were all nervous as it was so close to the Mozambique border, and they decided to move to just outside Mutare. Their new home was quite a distance from the so-called road and, very sadly, they were all beaten to death. A monument had been erected in their honour and on it were inscribed the words: 'My Father, I don't understand you/But I trust You'. There was a lot of sadness still about. Far too many holy and self-giving people were killed in vain, but their great work will not have been in vain. Finally, the bishop warned me to be careful as there were many landmines still about, even after 18 years.

At this stage I had only a couple of days left, but there were a number of engagements which I had not fulfilled. The Provincial Superior had organised an afternoon party for me which I considered a very kind gesture on her part. A number of Sisters attended and it was a lovely farewell. Other friends and lay people invited me to their homes but, unfortunately, time had run out. The very difficult part lay ahead of me, as I really dislike saying goodbye and the Sisters understood that. Many of my friends saw me off at the airport and their final gift to me was a large floral bouquet of Protea, the

South African emblem, which was greatly admired by my fellow passengers. I was sad to be leaving Zimbabwe where I had given many of the best years of my life in a beautiful country populated by such lovely, but hurting, people. I was sad because the Zimbabwe I had travelled to all those years ago had been a thriving commercial country, and what I saw now was a country desperately trying to go forward but sliding ever backwards, where intimidation, fear, hunger and poverty prevailed. However, I will always be grateful to the Sisters for their invitation and my prayers and thoughts will never be far from a people and country I dearly love.

While I was sad leaving, I had something special to look forward to on arrival and that, of course, was meeting Bill. When I arrived back in Ireland he was there, smiling and very happy to have me back home safely. I appreciated his warm welcome and his big hug. I happily settled into getting on with life back at home, until one day I got a bad fall in our backyard. Bill had called me to show me our two lovely white kittens playing behind the oil tank. I slipped and was taken by ambulance to Tralee General Hospital where I was very ill for a long time afterwards. When I was discharged from hospital I needed care, and my sister Eileen came to help us for a while. After a few weeks, Bill and I managed to get by, but the family continued to give assistance whenever we needed it. Due to this fall, I slowed down a bit and had to be content just doing work around the house. Bill was now working in the gardens at Glin Castle with Tom Wall, a job he still does and loves, because he has a real kinship with nature. He came home for lunch each day which kept me busy and broke up the day for me, and I also loved to hear about all the shrubs and flowers and birds in the gardens at Glin. Fortunately, after a while, I was able to start driving again and so could visit family and friends and go to daily Mass.

However, I had the misfortune of falling again a couple of years ago; this time it happened in our sitting room while I was watching a programme on television. It was a dance competition and one of the contestants was unable to dance, but kept winning. I was so annoyed that when I got up too quickly from the chair, I slipped and fell on the wooden floor. At first I thought I had damaged my coccyx, but later I discovered that I had fractured my pelvis in two places. Again I had to be hospitalised and had to rest for a substantial amount of time when I returned home. As a result of that fall I was very limited in the work I could do, both inside and outside the house. While this second fall limited my physical movement and freedom, the enforced rest gave me unexpected time and space to think about my life and the path it had taken.

I began to recollect my earlier years and the impulse that directed me to life as a missionary Sister, the challenge of leaving home at such a young age and setting off into a world that was totally unknown to me, the fulfilling work that I came to do in Zimbabwe, my return to Ireland and the unexpected joy at meeting Bill and getting married. I feel that I am one of the lucky ones with regard to the way my journey in life has unfolded. I believe that, in spite of the strict rules and the imposed silence and loneliness of those early years, my experiences have moulded my character into a positive and empathetic personality. My desire to go and work in Africa was fulfilled and, despite the problems encountered during and after the war years, I feel I have achieved much from a personal satisfaction point of view. It's nice to have a good start in life and I certainly had that in my native Direen. Likewise, it is nice to have a good ending and, considering that I am now a very happily married woman, living within a few miles of my birthplace, I have every reason to be grateful for the cards I was dealt in life and I hope I have played them to the best of my ability and honoured my calling.